S0-BTP-420

Laramie Junior High
1355 N 22nd
Laramie, WY 82070

The Sahara Desert

MANAGING EDITORS
Amy Bauman
Barbara J. Behm

CONTENT EDITORS
Amanda Barrickman
James I. Clark
Patricia Lantier
Charles P. Milne, Jr.
Katherine C. Noonan
Christine Snyder
Gary Turbak
William M. Vogt
Denise A. Wenger
Harold L. Willis
John Wolf

ASSISTANT EDITORS
Ann Angel
Michelle Dambeck
Barbara Murray
Renee Prink
Andrea J. Schneider

INDEXER
James I. Clark

ART/PRODUCTION
Suzanne Beck, Art Director
Andrew Rupniewski, Production Manager
Eileen Rickey, Typesetter

Copyright © 1992 Steck-Vaughn Company

Copyright © 1989 Raintree Publishers Limited Partnership
for the English language edition.

Original text, photographs and illustrations copyright ©
1985 Edizioni Vinicio de Lorentiis/Debate-Itaca.

All rights reserved. No part of the material protected by
this copyright may be reproduced or utilized in any form
by any means, electronic or mechanical, including photo-
copying, recording, or by any information storage and
retrieval system, without permission in writing from the
copyright owner. Requests for permission to make copies
of any part of the work should be mailed to: Copyright
Permissions, Steck-Vaughn Company, P.O. Box 26015,
Austin, TX 78755. Printed in the United States of America.

Library of Congress Number: 88-18337

2 3 4 5 6 7 8 9 0   97 96 95 94 93 92

Library of Congress Cataloging-in-Publication Data

Catalisano, Adelaide, 1956-
  [Sahara. English]
  The Sahara Desert / Adelaide Catalisano, Bruno Massa.

  — (World nature encyclopedia)
  Translation of: Sahara.
  Includes index.
  Summary: Describes the physical features, climate, and
plant and animal life of this North African desert.
  1. Desert ecology—Sahara—Juvenile literature. 2. Desert
biology—Sahara—Juvenile literature. [1. Desert ecology—
Sahara. 2. Desert biology—Sahara. 3. Sahara.] I. Massa,
Bruno, 1948-. II. Title. III. Series.
QH195.S3C3813   1988   574.5'.2652'0966—dc19   88-18331
ISBN 0-8172-3325-3

WORLD NATURE ENCYCLOPEDIA

The Sahara Desert

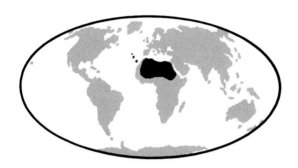

Adelaide Catalisano
Bruno Massa

Laramie Junior High
1355 N 22nd
Laramie, WY 82070

**RAINTREE
STECK-VAUGHN**
L I B R A R Y

Austin, Texas

CONTENTS

INTRODUCTION

The desert holds many secrets. The few people who study the desert for work or enjoyment are beginning to understand these secrets. This work takes great patience and skill. Except for the date palms and camels, there are few plants or animals that are easy to see. Understanding how they live in this immense scorching land of pebbles and sand is even more difficult.

To survive in such harsh conditions, all living things must find ways to obtain and conserve water and energy. Through evolutionary time, an organism changes in ways that make it better suited for the environment in which it lives. These methods of adaptation will be the main theme of this book.

The Sahara is the largest desert in the world. It stretches almost to the Mediterranean coast in northeast Africa. To the northwest in the region known as *Maghreb*, the Sahara stops at the Atlas Mountains. There is a strip of land along

this coast with a Mediterranean climate because it is separated from the desert by these mountains. In this journey through the Sahara, this unusual mountain chain that stands between Africa and Europe will be examined.

To complete any study of North Africa, it is essential to include a group of islands off the coast of northwest Africa. This group includes the Canary Islands, the Azores, and the Madeiras. In their biological makeup, they show the influence of both Africa and Europe. Some unusual species are called "endemic," which means they are found only on these islands. Islands often have plants and animals with unusual adaptations. These types of flora and fauna arise because the island species are cut off from the influences of life in other places. Ecologists call this condition "insularity." The effects of insularity on the Canary Islands, the Azores, and the Madeiras provide some fascinating examples of how living things grow.

THE DESERT

The driest lands on earth are found, for the most part, north of the equator. On the globe, these areas are located at approximately the same latitude as the Tropic of Cancer, between fifteen and forty degrees north of the equator. This belt of desert is composed of the Arabian Desert of Egypt, the deserts of the Middle East and Central Asia, the Sahara, and the deserts of North America. Although they are found at similar latitudes, the deserts are different from one another. Geographical locations create special conditions. Therefore, each desert is known for its particular climate, surface, and rock formations.

The Holarctic region is made up of the northern parts of the Old and New Worlds. This land contains the largest area of desert. Together with the southern deserts, these dry lands make up one-seventh of the entire planet's surface. The Sahara itself extends over more than 3,500,000 square miles (9,065,000 square kilometers). This huge expanse is approximately the size of the United States.

A Young Desert

The Sahara today is very different from what it was a few thousand years ago. At one time, great lakes covered huge areas of land, especially an area near Timbuktu, in the southwest Sahara. Today, there is no water in this area. For example, Lake Chad covered about 115,800 sq. miles (300,000 sq. km). Seven thousand years ago it began to recede until it covered only about 6,300 sq. miles (16,300 sq. km). Drought in the region has caused the lake to shrink even more. Now its size varies seasonally from 9,000 to 10,000 sq. miles (10,360 to 25,900 sq. km).

Five thousand years ago, the climate in the western Sahara was mild enough that large mammals could live off the plants that grew there. Evidence of these animals can be seen in the rock carvings. Also, large groups of birds migrated there for the winter months. Now these birds must fly over nearly 950 miles (1500 km) of desert to find areas with enough food and water for survival.

The vegetation of the Sahara, especially in the western regions, was mostly deciduous. In other words, the plants had leaves that fell off at the end of the growing season. The trees in the area were similar to those of Europe and the shrubs were similar to cypress and juniper. Overall, the appearance of the land was much like the savannah of today. There was a large, grassy plain with clusters of trees growing here and there.

Preceding pages: Pictured is a palm grove on the dunes of I-n-Salah in Algeria. Much of the Saharan lands known today originated in the last few thousand years. The arid regions have expanded continually and still do today. As the desert advances, the savannah life forms die out and are replaced by the few species of plants and animals that can tolerate extreme dryness.

Opposite page: Two pebbles that have been smoothed and rounded by the sand stand out on the reddish gold dunes of Habsasat in Morocco. The shifting sand of the desert or *erg* is the best known feature of the Sahara.

9

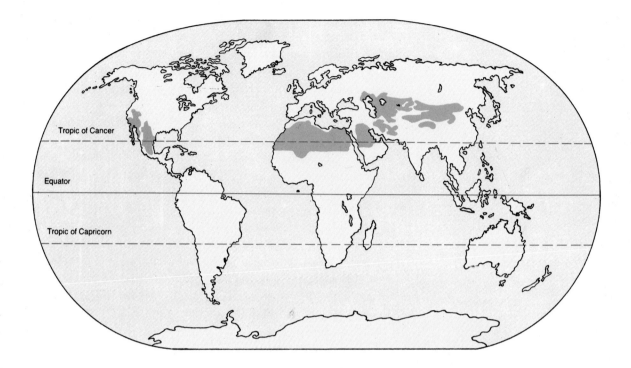

The arid lands of the northern regions, or Holarctic, form a kind of belt that roughly follows the Tropic of Cancer. Deserts other than the Sahara that are part of this strip are those in North America, central Asia, and the Arabian Peninsula. In the Southern Hemisphere, most of the deserts are found in Australia and southern Africa. As the sand continues to spread and as humans continue to exploit the soil, desert areas increase at a rate of 23,000 sq. miles (60,000 sq. km) a year.

For prehistoric people, the environment was a good one. Rock carvings show that early humans lived in the Sahara. Also, arrowheads and stone tools have been discovered. By studying the carvings, scientists have learned how animals followed one another as they moved from place to place. The western Sahara once contained lions, giraffes, elephants, crocodiles, and hippopotamuses. These animals originally came from Ethiopia. Today, because they could never survive crossing the desert, these species can no longer move into the regions that they once occupied.

Causes and Effects of Desert Formation

Deserts are defined climatically by the amount of precipitation that falls in the region. Precipitation is moisture in the form of rain, snow, hail, dew, and so on. True deserts receive less than 7.87 inches (200 millimeters) per year. This measurement, however, may be an average of several years' precipitation, because there are often long periods between rainfalls in the desert. In fact, the total rainfall for several years can occur in one night. In some parts of southern California, for example, it rains only every four or five years.

The desert regions in the latitudes close to the equator have regular winter and summer seasons. In these areas, the precipitation falls in a fairly even pattern.

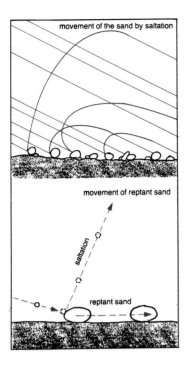

movement of the sand by saltation

movement of reptant sand

saltation

reptant sand

The wind is one of the atmospheric agents that causes the spectacular appearance of the desert. It transports and deposits the sand in two ways. Grains raised by a whirlwind fall in a curved pattern due to the wind's force and gravity. When they fall, the grains bounce back and the same forces carry them off again. This process is called saltation. With reptant sand, small grains are blown against larger ones, moving them with the wind.

The presence of mountains can affect rainfall and cause dry land. As clouds travel inland from the ocean, they can be stopped by a mountain chain. The clouds, which are heavy with rain, rise and cast a shadow on the ground below. Scientists call this the orographic (relating to mountains) shadow, or rain shadow. The clouds cool rapidly as they rise. Water vapor condenses into rain or snow and falls in the rain shadow. When the air passes to the other side of the mountain chain, it is very dry and rarely brings rain.

The desert is also known for the wide range of temperatures that occur daily. The temperatures are very high during the day and and very low at night. These extreme fluctuations are caused by the dry atmosphere. Moisture in the air acts as a filter. It protects the surface of the earth from the harsh rays of the sun. In the dry air of the desert, there is little moisture. The surfaces of the soil get very hot during the day. The soil loses heat rapidly at night because there is no moisture in the air to stop it from cooling. The temperatures then fall very low.

The appearance of the desert is affected by the wind and the small amount of precipitation that falls. The action of chemicals and other forces in the air can change the structure of rocks. However, because chemical agents need a certain amount of water, other forces, known as mechanical processes, take over in the desert.

One of these forces is the temperature range. During the hours of greatest exposure to the sun, or insolation, the surfaces of the rocks become very hot and expand. Some rocks expand more than others, depending on the temperature and the minerals they contain. At night, the temperature drops very low and the surfaces of the rocks contract. The expansion and contraction of the rocks each day causes them to split and crumble.

Other forces in the environment speed the crumbling of the rocks. During periods of heavy rainfall, the rocks expand from the water that is absorbed by minerals in the rocks. Also, minerals can penetrate the rocks from the air through oxidization, which occurs when a substance combines with oxygen. Another force that affects the rocks is the wind. Crystals of salt are carried by the wind and penetrate the openings in the rock.

Finally, there are the desert rains. Though they are brief, the rains generally pour down in torrents. The water runs quickly across the surface of rock and sweeps away small fragments. The waters wash away the soil and cut

A spectacular view of the Ahaggar Mountains in the Algerian Sahara. This great desert region is famous not only because of its beautiful scenery but also because it is fairly easy to reach. Tamanrasset is the capital of the region and is connected to Algeria by a long asphalt road. Today, people can travel from the Mediterranean coast into the heart of the desert in a few hours. The base of the mountain range is approximately 185,000 sq. miles (480,000 sq. km), which is about as large as Colorado and Utah. The mountains appeared following violent volcanic eruptions during the Tertiary or Quaternary periods.

deeply into the rock, creating narrow mountain gorges. In this way, the heavy rainfalls contribute to the process of erosion.

Deflation is the name geologists have given to the action of the wind that erodes the soil. Wind erosion occurs more in deserts than in humid areas. This is because there is little vegetation to keep the soil in place and because of the dryness. Without moisture to weigh them down, particles of fine soil are carried by the wind high into the air. The wind may scatter them even beyond the desert area. The wind blows the heavier grains of sand over the surface of the

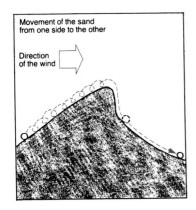

Movement of the sand from one side to the other

Direction of the wind

rocks. These sands slowly wear away the rocks. Tiny particles come loose from the rock and become part of the sand that blows in the desert. In this way, new sand is constantly formed. The erosive power of the wind can be seen in the shapes of the rocks themselves. They have a rounded, mushroom shape because the wind has smoothed all the rough corners and eroded them, mainly at their base.

The wind is not merely destructive. Its force also creates the dunes, one of the desert's most spectacular features.

The grains of sand rise into the air and are carried until they fall when the wind dies or they meet an obstacle. As the grains fall, the sands build up, forming another obstacle. The wind deposits more sand causing a pile to form. This pile is known as a dune. As the wind blows in various directions, it shapes the surface of the desert almost like the sea. The hills and valleys continually change, depending on the force and direction of the wind.

If the vegetation does not hold them back, the dunes move in the direction of the prevailing winds. When the wind blows on one side of the dune, the other side is protected.

The wind moves the grains of sand up the first side and over the top to the other side. There they are protected from the wind, and the movement of the sands stops. The sand continues to shift in this way from the unprotected side to the protected side. The erg is a sand formation in the Sahara that is formed this way. Ergs are huge sandbanks and spectacular dunes that often have a crescent shape. This crescent, or *barchans*, is formed by the force of the wind on the sand. The sand in the middle resists the wind more than the sand on the sides. This unequal resistance to the wind forms the crescent of the barchans. The continual movement of the dunes stops when there is a rainfall. Plant life springs up on the dune, anchoring the sand around it.

Geography of the Desert

Many countries share the Sahara Desert. From west to east, there are Western Sahara, Mauritania, southern Morocco, a large part of Algeria, southern Tunisia, and most of Libya and Egypt. The southern Sahara includes parts of Sudan, Chad, Niger, and Mali. This desert extends over a surface of more than 3,500,000 sq. miles (9,065,000 sq. km) and, at its longest point, stretches almost 2,800 miles (4,500 km) both from north to south and east to west.

Sand dunes in the Algerian Sahara. This landscape is beautiful to look at but is a very difficult land in which to survive. Some small animals manage to survive here by hiding from the scorching sun under an inch or two of sand.

Though its landscape can be monotonous, the Sahara offers some variety. There are sections, known as *reg*, that are covered with pebbles. Other areas, known as *hammada*, are flat, windswept surfaces of rock. There also are the huge sand dunes previously mentioned known as erg. There are isolated, mountainous areas with steep cliffs and large, scattered boulders that jut out from the landscape. Ancient riverbeds that once were the water transport system of the area still can be seen. These *wadis*, which means "river" in Arabic, are dry through most of the year. The riverbeds are clues that this area had a more temperate climate in the past. They also indicate that the land had more life-forms than presently exist.

Today, travelers may enter the western Sahara only by three main routes: Algeria-Tamanrasset, Algeria-Djanet, and Oran-Béchar. But the people who live in the area say that in the beginning of the twentieth century, it was possible to cross the Sahara on horseback from southern Morocco near Goulimine to Senegal. Travel was easier because at that time wide grasslands existed along the Atlantic coast where now only desert is found.

Pictured is the bed of a dry river ("wadi") near Tripoli. Rivers in the desert contain little water. What water there is evaporates quickly in the dry air. As a result, the waterways usually dry up at some point in the huge desert. In some cases, however, the water in the subsoil allows grasses and trees to grow. Other wadis can be found that are actually "fossilized" riverbeds, which contained water for thousands of years.

A sandstorm rages against sparse herds in northern Niger. The most common Saharan wind is the *ghibli*. It blows north from deep inside the desert and causes an intolerable increase in temperature and a decrease in humidity. Other winds that stir up violent sandstorms are the *khamsin* and the *harmattan*.

Today, that vegetation has disappeared. Dromedaries, which are a type of camel, are the only beasts of burden that can live for long in this environment. In recent times, the Sahara Desert has advanced due to natural causes and the influence of people. The Sahara now completely separates the Palearctic (northern, non-desert) regions from central Africa, including Ethiopia.

In northeast Africa, the desert occupies a huge area. It extends from thirty degrees north latitude, where at one point it almost touches the Mediterranean coast, south to Chad and northern Sudan, in north central Africa. In the east, the desert extends from nineteen degrees east longitude to the Red Sea. Only the Nile Valley breaks the continuous desert in this region.

In Libya, the desert reaches the Mediterranean coast. However, in Cyrenaica, a region in eastern Libya, there is high land reaching to about 1,640 feet (500 meters). Because of this altitude, desert conditions do not dominate, and Cyrenaica enjoys a Mediterranean climate.

LIFE
IN THE DESERT

The Saharan climate is one of the most hostile that can be imagined for living organisms. Throughout the year, the temperatures vary greatly. In some interior regions, such as the Great Eastern Erg in Algeria, weather station records show winter night temperatures of 14° Fahrenheit (-10° Celsius). Summer daytime temperatures can reach 112°F (50°C) in the shade. Many animal and plant species cannot stand temperature ranges of this kind. Not only are the temperatures severe, but the humidity drops as low as 4 to 5 percent. Such low humidity causes intense evaporation and transpiration, or loss of water through the skin.

Everyone knows that rain is a rare event in the desert. As mentioned earlier, areas where the rainfall is less than 7.87 inches (200 mm) of rain per year are defined as deserts. Yet, less than half that amount, about 4 inches (100 mm), falls in the Sahara each year.

Desert winds occur much more often than the rain. They blow from so many directions and have so many different characteristics that they are given special names. One typical Saharan wind is called the *khamsin*. This wind blows from the south-southwest in the spring for about fifty days. When this violent wind blows, there are great sand-storms and the temperature rises quickly. Another wind is the *ghibli*, which means "south" in Arabic. This hot wind usually comes at night and without warning. It arises in the interior regions and blows northward for several days. The ghibli brings extremely dry air and hot temperatures. The *harmattan* is a hot, dry wind that comes from the equator and blows in an east-west direction for two to six days. This choking wind is filled with dust, sand, and other objects from the soil that may be carried as far as Cape Verde and the Canary Islands.

As the temperature range and the wind mold the desert through the processes of erosion, the desert itself molds its inhabitants. Living things must either fight the climate or avoid its harshness. They are forced to develop a series of adaptations necessary for survival. These adaptations may be physiological (related to how the body or parts of a living thing function) or behavioral (related to how a living thing acts under certain conditions). Access to water is the first and most important problem that desert organisms must face. Because of the high temperature and low humidity, both plants and animals lose large amounts of water through transpiration. To survive, living organisms have developed many different solutions to this problem.

Opposite page: Acacias near Atar (Mauritania) are pictured. Desert plants have undergone extreme adaptations to gather and save water in spite of seemingly impossible conditions. Only about one thousand species have been able to adapt to conditions in the Sahara. Among these plants are annual herbaceous (green, not woody) plants, shrubs, succulents, and some trees.

Plants: Problems and Adaptations

If deserts were irrigated, drought, which keeps desert plants from growing, would be eliminated. Then the desert lands could become highly productive. The amount of light is plentiful so there is no competition among plants for it, as there is in the forest. To survive in very dry or in arid zones is always very hard for plants. They struggle each day to get water. Life in these places is so hard that in the Sahara Desert only about a thousand plant species are known. This number is very small considering the vast area that the desert covers.

A few plants survived because they changed in some way and adapted to the drought-stricken land. They also developed mechanisms that allow them to stop the growth of possible competitors. The spacing of individual plants is a clue to the survival of some species. Often there are empty stretches of land between plants. As they grow, the plants keep these spaces open by means of an antibiotic produced in their roots. This antibiotic prevents the development of seeds in nearby plants. This adaptation gives the plant a large surface from which it can absorb water. It does not have to compete with other plants for the nearby moisture.

Shown is a flowering leguminous (bearing pods with seeds) plant on a sand dune. Sometimes the seeds of the desert plants survive several years of drought and then sprout rapidly when conditions become favorable.

Pictured are tufts of grass in an arid region of Algeria. Desert plants often are spaced in surprisingly regular fashion. This pattern allows them to exploit the extremely scarce water in the subsoil.

Among the desert plants, the annuals are most common. These grow, flower, and die in one year or one season. To avoid drought, they grow only where there is enough moisture. Their life cycle is very short. Species have been discovered that grow, flower, and die in only eight hours. The parts of these plants that grow above ground show no special signs of adaptation to the desert. The seeds, however, are an excellent example of survival strategies. They can remain inactive, or dormant, for long periods of drought, which may last several years. When water becomes available, they may suddenly sprout.

However, the amount of water that swells and breaks the coverings of the seeds must be enough for the plant to go through its whole life cycle. The plant sprouts only when it is certain of being able to complete such a cycle.

Many annual plants are xerophytes. The structure of these plants is adapted for life and growth with a limited water supply. They are the most common plants in deserts. In the Sahara, forty-two species of xerophytes are known. They are absent in humid tropical climates. In subtropical and temperate climates, fewer than fifteen species are

Dromedaries are shown drinking at a "guelta" (spring). As did the Bactrian camels, these animals probably came from the arid regions of Asia and reached North Africa with the nomads. Dromedaries and Bactrian camels, which were domesticated in very ancient times, continue to be necessary for people who live in the desert. Today, every herd of dromedaries is owned by someone, just as reindeers are owned by the inhabitants of extreme northern regions. Most Bactrian camels, except for a few herds in the Gobi Desert, also live under the care of people.

known and the Arctic contains fewer than five known species.

Perennials are plants that survive for long periods and flower several times. Shrubs and bulbs are examples of perennials. The shrubs have small, thick leaves that drop off during severe drought. In this way, the plant avoids withering by returning the moisture that would have escaped through the leaves' pores (stomata). The bulbs remain inactive for most of the year. They have a thick network of roots. These run through the surface layers of the soil and can take advantage of the night humidity.

Of the perennial plants, the succulents have the most complex adaptive mechanism. The cactus family is the best-known member of the succulents. They have no leaves and are just a large stem. This shape limits the surface through which water can be lost to transpiration. The stem expands and becomes an excellent place to store water. The plant can survive long periods of drought by drawing on this water that it stored during the rains.

The surface of these plants is also very small. They have a rounded or spherical shape to reduce the surface area in contact with the air. The stem is covered with thick cuticles (external, protective layers). There are very few stomata, which reduces evaporation as much as possible. The cacti and opuntias of the American deserts and the spurges of the African deserts are succculents with these features.

Because succulent plants have no leaves, the chlorophyll that causes their characteristic green color is found in the stem and exterior tissues. Non-desert plants need light to produce their food. Daytime, however, is the hottest time in the desert and plants would lose precious water through stomata if they were active at this time. Most of the succulents undergo "crassulacae acid metabolism" (CAM). This special kind of photosynthesis can occur in the dark and needs light only in the last stages. This adaptation allows plants to make food during the cooler temperatures of the night when less moisture will escape.

In the great ergs of the Sahara and in other sandy soils *drinn* is found. It is a grass with a long, branched rhizome (horizontal plant stem). When the dune systems are very large, the drinn grows near a shrubby vegetation formed by the nearly leafless ephedras and Saharan broom. Among the grasses, the *Danthonia fragilis* grows abundantly.

The rocky desert soil is characterized by another endemic species, the peculiar *Fredolia aretioides*. This plant spreads over vast areas where it is the only vegetation. Compact tufts form its surface. It is shaped like a half-circle and may be more than 20 inches (50 centimeters) in diameter. Its branches grow very close together, and the spaces between them are filled in by sand blown by the wind. Its leaves are very compact and hard.

Animals: Physiological Adaptations

The animals of the arid lands also have developed adaptations to the dry climate and the scarce water supply.

A gerbil appears near its den in the Libyan desert south of Tripoli. Desert rodents are generally nocturnal because they cannot survive the direct rays of the sun during the day. They can, however, sometimes be seen outside their underground tunnels in the cooler hours of the early morning, the late afternoon, or on cloudy days in fall and winter.

Some animals that are able to move around easily can avoid water loss by leaving the dry lands. They move or migrate to areas where the desert is receiving rains at the time. These migrations, however, are not always successful. Many migrating gazelles and antelope have died on their journey to find water. Various traces of their unfortunate treks can be seen along the usual paths to the areas with a supply of water.

Another way of surviving dry conditions is to remain in the desert and adapt to the climate. Reptiles and insects do just that and are the species that have adapted best to living in the most arid zones. Both groups have a very thick exterior cover (integument). Also, their excretions are solid and almost dry. They contain a lot of uric acid and guanine (a nitrogen compound found in animal waste and nitrogen fixing plants, or legumes). Insects also secrete waxy sub-

stances. Water vapor cannot pass through them, so water loss is kept down. Finally, metabolic water, or water in the insect's body that is used for its life processes, is also saved. Darkling beetles (a name that refers to their nighttime, or nocturnal, habits) can even increase the amount of metabolic water they make through special bodily functions.

Some desert mammals are able to save water so well that they live only on the moisture produced by their own breathing. The desert jerboa is one of the best-adapted desert mammals. Its adaptations begin inside its body. The large intestine is adapted for reabsorbing water from its waste materials. In fact, its solid waste, or feces, is almost entirely without water.

When they breathe, jerboas show another evolutionary adaptation. Air that moves through the nasal passages is cooled and condensed, so that little moisture escapes. It is

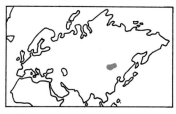

Today, the dromedary *(top)* and the Bactrian camel *(bottom)* are the only two representatives of the camel family from the Old World. The one-humped dromedary is widespread in western Asia and North Africa. The two-humped Bactrian camel is used as a beast of burden in many desert areas of Asia.

Opposite page: Pictured are two dromedaries in the huge dunes of Beni Abbès, Algeria. The hooves of these animals have two cushioned toes that do not sink into the sand. This makes travel through the desert easier.

possible because the temperature of the tissue inside the nose is lower than the normal body temperature. The water that is exhaled with the warm air from the lungs condenses and stays inside the nasal passages. As the desert jerboa inhales dry air, the moisture contained in its nasal ducts evaporates. The nose is cooled, and the incoming air is saturated with water. This humidified air is exhaled from the lungs, but the majority of the water in the exhaled air condenses and is stored in the nasal ducts. In this way, the little rodent alternates evaporation with condensation and keeps water loss from breathing to a minimum.

Another problem that desert animals must solve is controlling the amount of salt in the body. Animals take in a large amount of salt with their food. Some of it must be eliminated in order to keep a certain level of salt in their bodies. It is very important that the animal be able to excrete salt through the kidneys. When a lot of water is available, the animal excretes the salt in its urine. But when water is scarce, the animal saves the water that would become urine. As a result, salt builds up in the urine.

The role of the kidneys is to reabsorb the water that would be lost in the urine. It is clear that the saving of water by the kidneys is essential for desert animals.

By dissecting a jerboa, it can be seen that their kidneys are equipped with long collecting tubules. These tubules keep water from being excreted as urine. In comparison, mammals living in habitats with adequate water have short tubules. Humans have shorter tubules than jerboas. They also have about four times more salt in the urine than in the blood. Jerboas, with their long tubules, have eight times as much salt in their urine as is in their blood.

When land animals metabolize protein and other compounds containing nitrogen, there is nitrogen left over that the body does not use. Land animals excrete nitrogen in the form of complex organic molecules, such as urea. Urea must be dissolved in order to be eliminated. Therefore, in areas where water is scarce, valuable water can be lost in this way.

Reptiles and birds eliminate nitrogen in the form of uric acid. This acid forms crystals that do not dissolve in water. Therefore, uric acid can be eliminated with little loss of water. Because of this adaptation, the reptiles and birds are the most active of desert vertebrates. They can move about even during the warmest hours of the day, when loss of water is the greatest.

Several thousand years ago, two populations of camels

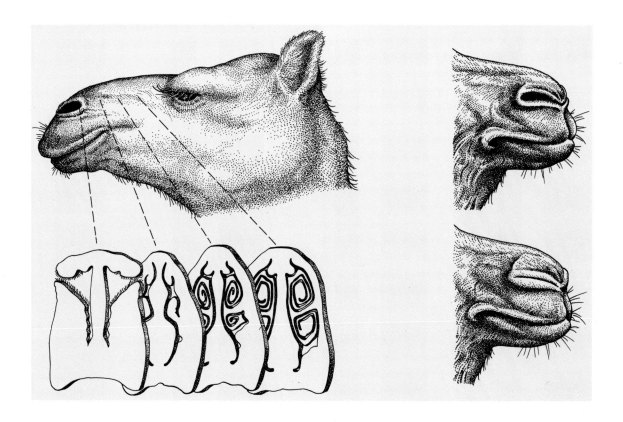

became geographically separated and developed different characteristics. The two-humped Bactrian camel lived in central Asia, and the one-humped camel, the dromedary, lived in Arabia. It is not known when the dromedary last lived in the wild. According to biblical texts, it has been a companion of human beings for more than four thousand years.

After these animals were domesticated, an entire civilization of nomads used them as beasts of burden in journeying from the Asian deserts to the western Sahara. The dromedary moved from Arabia to Africa around A.D. 1200, when conditions in Egypt and Mesopotamia made it possible for them to survive the journey. For thousands of years populations of nomadic Arabs, Bedouins, marauders, shepherds, and hunters have built their lives around the camel.

The success of the dromedary as a desert animal is based on important physiological and anatomical adaptations. First, it is an ungulate artiodactyl, that is, a hoofed animal with two toes. The toes are covered with fleshy pads or cushions. This adaptation reduces friction with the sand and protects the feet from the heat of the desert soil. The two

Top left: The camel's nose contains spiral or scroll-shaped structures. These structures increase the surface area in contact with the air. Precious water can be reabsorbed from the air that the camel exhales.

Top right: When necessary, the Bactrian camel and the dromedary can open and close their nostrils by using special muscles. This adaptation is extremely useful in sandstorms.

25615

LJHS-1995   574.5/WOR   15.00

Below: Illustrated is a fringe-toed lizard emerging from its hole. Fringe-toed lizards are typical of arid zones and are found in southern Spain as well as in Africa and Asia.

Below right: Shown are the numerous footprints and tracks left by a small lizard around the opening to its hole in the Algerian erg (sand desert).

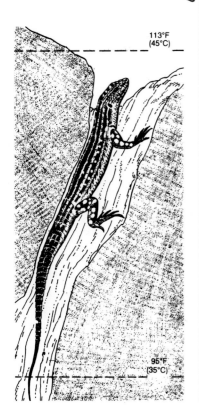

113°F
(45°C)

95°F
(35°C)

cushions form a single large surface. The amount of weight on each surface is reduced, and the camel does not sink.

The structure of their feet allows Bactrian camels and dromedaries to cross more than 62 miles (100 km) of desert in only a day. Their eyes and noses also are well adapted to life in sandy places. When sandstorms are blowing furiously, camels protect themselves by flexing muscles that open and close the nostrils. Their long eyelashes protect their eyes from sand particles carried by the wind.

All warm-blooded animals must maintain a certain body temperature. When it is very hot, they sweat and pant to lower their body temperature. Evaporation of sweat uses heat, which helps to lower their temperature. The dromedary is active during the day. It must save as much water as possible and so must use some way other than sweating to keep down its temperature. Its body is covered with a layer of soft wool. A cushion of air is trapped in the wool and acts as a barrier to the sun's strong rays. In addition, because the camel has a higher temperature than most mammals, there is not such a great difference between the animal's temperature and that of the environment.

During long desert trips, dromedaries obtain the water

Laramie Junior High
1355 N 22nd
Laramie, WY 82070

Pictured is a stylized figure of a lion in rock at Taghit, Algeria. These works of unknown artists clearly indicate that thousands of years ago, a savannah climate, with all its typical animals, dominated this region. There were lions, antelope, giraffes, and even crocodiles. It is believed that crocodiles lived in the little ponds among the scattered oases as recently as a century ago.

they need from eating green vegetation and spiny shrubs. Many desert plants have spines as a defense against plant-eating animals (herbivores). However, the thorny surfaces do not bother the tough mouth and tongue of the camel.

Dromedaries also produce and store a large quantity of fat in their humps. When food and water are scarce, these animals use this fat as a source of water. When the fat is broken down, water is formed. Additional water is provided by special water-bearing cavities, or alveoli, present in the stomach. Under extreme conditions, camels or dromedaries can lose up to one-fourth of their weight. However, they can gain it back quickly by taking in food and, most importantly, water. Camels may consume as much as 26 gallons (100 liters) at one time.

In most cases, desert animals are active at dawn, twilight, and night. This behavior allows them to avoid unnecessary and dangerous exposure to the sun. During the day,

Many birds can be found in Saharan oases. The black-headed bush shrike of the savannah and open forest lives at lush oases. The Namaqua dove, a small member of the order of Columbiformes (sand grouses, pigeons, and doves), is found in the dry savannahs of a large part of Africa and at the southern limits of the Sahara. The Barbary partridge, typically Mediterranean, is widespread in the Maghreb, Cyrenaica, Sardinia, and in an isolated area in Tassili between Algeria and Libya.

black-headed bush shrike

Namaqua dove

Barbary partridge

desert animals try to find shelter from the hot sun. Some hide under rocky crags. Others, such as rodents and reptiles, go underground where it is cool and moist. Their holes may be only a few inches deep. Compared to the dry, burning heat on the surface, though, it is a different world underground. In a sense, these animals create their own climates.

Whether it is winter or summer, the temperature and humidity in burrows stay at an even level. In the winter, the temperature in the burrow may be warmer than the air on the surface. In the summer, the burrow is cooler. During the hot seasons, these animals go out only at dawn, twilight, and night. The temperature on the surface is as cool as the burrow at those times. In the cooler season, the animals go out during the warmer, midday hours.

Though they have the cover of darkness, nocturnal animals are not safe when they come out of their holes at night. Predators hunt at night. They track rodents, reptiles, and other animals by using their keen sense of smell. They also see well in the dark. Birds depend more on their keen sight for night hunting, while mammals depend on their sense of smell.

The Journey of Heim de Balsac

About fifty years ago, a wave of explorers and settlers pushed into Africa. With them were European naturalists who led expeditions. Their travels produced a large amount of interesting and useful information about the life of desert animals. Today, people who study the desert still use those findings in their research.

One of these explorers was the French ornithologist (one who studies birds) Heim de Balsac. He identified many species and left a detailed account of his adventures. De Balsac entered the western Sahara in 1930.

The information collected by Heim de Balsac in his long journey is valuable today. Naturalists can trace the history and dynamics of the advance of the desert by comparing his findings with more recent data. His notes on the geographical distribution of some species are especially useful. For example, Balsac indicated that certain birds common to dry, but not completely desert, areas lived in a specific place. Today, that species no longer lives there. The deduction is that the desert has advanced. Desert species such as the sand grouse or hoopoe lark are common today but were not in de Balsac's time. This finding also suggests that the desert now covers land that it once did not.

SURVIVAL STRATEGIES: INVERTEBRATES, AMPHIBIANS, AND REPTILES

The desert supports a much smaller amount of living material for each foot, yard, or mile of space than other environments. Even so, a surprising number of animals, mammals, birds, reptiles, invertebrates, and even fish and amphibians live in the desert. Most of these animals are much smaller than species living in more hospitable environments. Because they are small, these animals need less water and food. They also more easily find shelter from the sun's rays. Dehydration still remains a great danger. Small creatures must have special mechanisms to protect themselves from water loss. Invertebrates such as insects, arachnids (includes spiders), and crustaceans (includes scorpions), have an external cuticle or waxy covering. Water vapor cannot pass through this cuticle.

Desert Invertebrates

Of all the animal species, the best desert survivors are the insects and spiders. They belong to a group known as arthropods. These small but numerous animals are found both on land and in water. A peculiar characteristic is their very strong shell or cuticle. Under the extreme temperatures in the desert, the cuticle thickens and becomes hardened.

In the Sahara, arthropods take many strange forms. Scorpions are very common and have a body with two parts. The anterior (front) has two appendages that end in strong pincers. The posterior (rear) ends in a large tail with a poison sting. The scorpion has two large eyes and two sets of smaller eyes in the anterior part of its shield-like covering. Inside its stomach, the scorpion has other sensing organs called combs. They are made up of a series of thin flat scales, membranes, or layers called lamellae which are laid one above the other like tiles.

Scorpions are nocturnal. During the day they stay sheltered under the sand or stones. They wait for other arthropods or small animals to come near enough to grab with their pincers. They inject venom only if it is necessary to paralyze the prey. The venom of some Saharan scorpions can be deadly, even for humans. The poison of other, less dangerous scorpions causes irritation, pain, swelling, and temporary paralysis where the stinger enters.

A familiar sight in the Sahara is the animal that the Arabs call the "wind scorpion." It is a speedy, nocturnal arthropod that looks like a scorpion. This animal also is called the "false spider" and the "sun spider." Scientists call them solfugids, which is the name of the family to which

Opposite page: The African spiny-tailed lizard is one of the most common desert saurians. It belongs to a genus widespread in North Africa and in Asia. This robust reptile can reach about 16 inches (40 cm) in length and weigh over 1 pound (.5 kg). Its large, spiny tail holds a reserve of water and fat to use during dry periods.

these arthropods belong. For its size, the solfugid's pincers are enormous. They hold the prey while the solfugid chews. Two other appendages grow near the mouth. These are called pedipalps and look like hairy legs. The pedipalps move the prey back and forth as the solfugid chews. Because of the pedipalps, the sun spider appears to have ten legs instead of eight.

Its yellowish body is covered by many hairs, which have a sensory function. The wind scorpion preys on other arthropods. Though its bite can be painful to humans, it is not poisonous. The mating of these animals is unique. The male attacks the female. She remains motionless as he turns her over on her back and injects a drop of seminal fluid into her genital pore.

Crickets and grasshoppers, members of the order Orthoptera, are among the most widespread insect species in the Sahara. One unusual cricket is a shiny yellowish color with wings and large jaws protruding from its relatively big head. It can be heard more easily than seen. The cricket makes a high frequency shrieking or chirping sound

This Saharan scorpion grows to about 4 inches (10 cm) long. It can be very harmful to humans. It has a painful sting that injects a poison, which is toxic to the nervous system. Severe swelling occurs where the person has been stung. Fever, hallucinations, and other serious disorders can follow. Cases of death are rare if the person stung is an adult and in good health.

Sacred scarabs busily roll a ball of dung mixed with earth and sand. The female deposits an egg inside the ball and then buries it carefully in a hole. The organic material in the ball is a rich store of food for the single larva that hatches from the egg.

as it stands at the entrance of its home. The cricket's body only partly comes out of the hole so it can withdraw quickly in case of danger.

The migratory locusts are the best-known grasshoppers because they cause so much damage to the vegetation. Swarms as large as 155 miles (250 km) long and 12 miles (20 km) wide have been seen during their greatest invasions. Once nearly 2,000 sq. miles (5,000 sq. km) of crops were destroyed in five days. Another time locusts in Morocco devoured seven thousand tons of oranges in five days.

During their life cycles, locusts pass through a number of phases. In the solitary phase, they live alone. In the gregarious phase, they live in groups. Then this pattern reverses itself. One entomologist (a person who studies insects) observed these animals for most of his life. He discovered that the solitary locusts became gregarious in a few generations when they had frequent contact with other locusts. Their features and physiology (how organisms function in life) also changed.

Locusts develop an insatiable hunger and are extremely resistant to thirst when they are gregarious. They are able to produce water from ingested plant material. These hardy insects can survive desert soil temperatures as high as

35

The guelta (spring) of Afilale in the Ahaggar Mountains of Algeria is shown. In these dry regions, thick vegetation grows very quickly where underground water finds a way to the surface. Many animal species that depend on these springs for survival gather near them. The photograph looks like the Saharan oases before people began bringing in species such as the date palm, the common banana, the common fig, the pomegranate, and others for cultivation.

140°F (60°C) in the sun. Such a temperature would kill any other animal. Locusts survive because their exoskeleton (external supportive covering) allows moisture to pass through. Their metabolic water passes through the surface of their bodies, evaporates, and cools them.

There are many species of desert beetle with very thick exoskeletons. The most common are large ground beetles that grow to about 2 inches (5 cm) long. They can be recognized by their shiny, black bodies with wide, white spots. These beetles can be observed during the evening and the cooler parts of the day as they run along sandy and stony soil. At other times, they seek shelter under bushes or stones.

The sacred scarab beetle is common in the desert. It is often found along the dromedary routes. This insect is a scavenger that feeds on the droppings of other animals. It collects its food by rolling a piece of dung into a ball with its back legs. The scarab beetle was worshipped by the ancient Egyptians, who thought of the dung ball as a symbol of the world and resurrection. The notched crown on the beetle's head was symbolic of the rising sun to them.

The beetle was an important part of the ceremony when the Egyptians mummified their dead. They removed the heart of the dead person and replaced it with a carved scarab. The beetle represented resurrection.

The sacred scarab takes particular care of its young. It lays a single egg in a long sphere of dung. Then it carefully buries the dung. The newly hatched larva finds enough food in the dung ball to grow and change to its adult form. Scarab beetles are most active during the warm hours and fly best in warm temperatures.

Amphibians: Either Water or Death

From time to time, oases appear in the desert. In these temporary water sources live a few fish and amphibians that show very interesting adaptations to life in the desert. When the pools dry out, these animals bury themselves in the damp ground and wait for better weather.

Among the most beautiful stories recounting the life of these unusual animals is one by the naturalist Giuseppe Scortecci. He described how panther toads of the Ghāt Oasis face the difficult period of sandstorms. "After the tenth of March, the air began to darken, the wind began blowing harder and harder, and the temperature rose. On the thirteenth day, the air became so dry that it was very painful to stay outside for long. In the middle of the day,

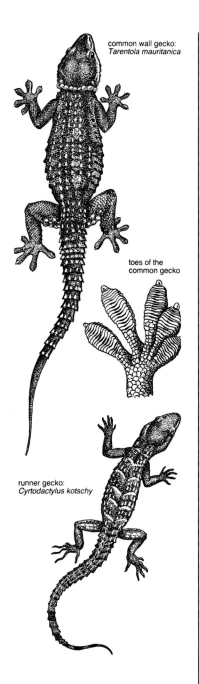

common wall gecko:
Tarentola mauritanica

toes of the common gecko

runner gecko:
Cyrtodactylus kotschy

The gecko family is subdivided into two groups based on form and structure differences. These differences arise from the groups' diverse life-styles. For example, the toes of common geckos have pads with microscopic hooks that adhere to any surface. The toes of *Cyrtodactylus kotschy,* on the other hand, have claws. The latter's body is flattened.

when the ghibli was at its peak, I wrapped my head in a *smala,* put on a pair of glasses and left the fort where I was lodging. The wind forced me to stay bent over and at times even to crawl on my hands and knees in order not to be knocked down. Sand penetrated the cloth and went into my mouth. . . . I knew the toads used to hide on the margins of ditches, in the holes they dug, and that thousands of small larvae crowded the pools. I looked for them.

"Digging in the sand in places where not much earlier the reservoirs had been, I found lumps made of the dead bodies of the larvae. Digging on the edges of the ditches and searching in the shelters of the panther toads, I found many to be empty, some with two or three individuals already dried out, others overpopulated. The croaking creatures that a few days earlier I had seen overcome by love, intoxicated with life, and longing to create new life, now formed great tangles with their bodies. They held onto each other, the males making use of their suction pads to hold onto another's trunk, a fat thigh, or a large, warty head.

"Those that formed the outer layer of the tangle were dead and desiccated (dried up), those in the second layer were in a sad condition, and those in the center, two or three individuals at the most, were alive, but in a state of extreme torpor (inactive and stiff)."

The sandstorm kills all the panther toads in its path. However, the dried out bodies of the victims protect a few toads who survive the storm. When calm returns, a loud croaking rises from the pools of the oases. It sounds like a cry of victory because some of the toads have won their battle against a forbidding environment.

Reptiles of the Sahara

Between 65 and 225 million years ago during the Mesozoic era, great numbers of reptiles lived on earth. They dwelt in many different habitats—in caves, on the ground, in water, and in trees. Some of these reptiles lived in the area occupied today by the Sahara Desert. At that time, this land was covered with great expanses of forest. Today, reptiles still play an important role in desert life. They have adapted magnificently to the many environmental changes that the land has undergone.

One way they protect themselves from the heat is by hiding in underground holes or in rocky ravines during the day. They also have scaly skin to protect them from water loss. Finally, they are able to obtain water from the plants

and animals they eat. Lizards feed mostly on insects, while snakes have a wider variety of food sources. They eat insects, small mammals, other reptiles, and small birds.

All lizards that have ever existed are grouped under the name *saurians*. Of these, geckos have adapted particularly well to the desert. Most of them have survived by becoming nocturnal. Zoologists separate them into two groups. First are the wall geckos. They have small pads with numerous microscopic hooks under the toes. These pads help them cling to any surface. The second type exhibits different behavior and has toes that are adapted for running quickly. Both groups have large eyes that help them hunt at night. With their large jaws, geckos are able to catch fairly large prey. In general, they hunt insects, spiders, and other arthropods, including small scorpions. Geckos also have a remarkable ability to conserve water in their tails.

Other common desert reptiles are the small, fringe-toed lizards. They can change color rapidly to blend into their background. They also can run quickly on their hind legs. Their speed, however, does not save them from being food

An elegant skink is one of the saurians best adapted to life in the sandy desert. The wedge-shaped snout is very useful for digging. The smooth and almost porcelain-like scales help it to slide rapidly through tunnels that collapse as soon as it passes. Its color gives it almost perfect camouflage during the brief time it spends above ground.

An agama in the rocky desert is shown.
Agamas vary somewhat in shape, size,
and habits, but all are agile. Many
species of these insectivorous saurians
live in Asia and Africa, including the
Sahara.

for predators. Another species adapted to life in the desert is the common skink. This small, agile saurian moves quickly over the sand. Its body is robust, rounded, and completely covered by a layer of very smooth, shiny scales.

The skink's nose is pointed or shovel-like. It extends out over a recessed or set-back mouth (see photograph). This design protects its mouth from sand when the skink digs. The legs of the common skink are well developed. Other skinks that live below the soil have legs that have atrophied, or withered, from disuse. The common skink is very active during the warmest hours of the day. When searching for prey, it moves as if swimming through the sand. Orthopterons (winged insects), beetles, and centipedes are its main foods. Enemies of the common skink include monitor lizards. People use it as food or dry it to use as medicine.

Opposite page: Jacobson's organ is a
true "sixth sense," a blend of taste and
touch. This organ is well developed in
snakes and monitors. These reptiles
continuously "taste" the ground,
vibrating their long tongues in search of
possible prey.

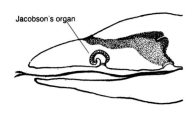
Jacobson's organ

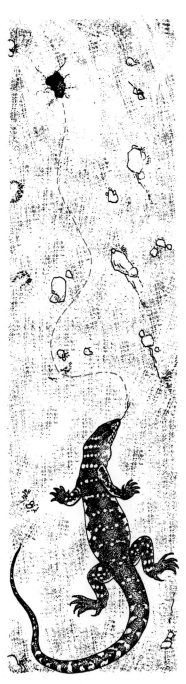

The monitors were named terrestrial (land) crocodiles by the Greek historian Herodotus. These large saurians are so adaptable that they are found in a variety of environments. This species is widespread along the desert strip that runs from the western Sahara all the way to Pakistan.

The desert monitor is a typical diurnal (active in the day) animal. It becomes most active when the sun is at its highest and the air is hot. Using its powerful legs, the monitor runs very rapidly. It also has extremely strong claws, which it uses for digging.

These large lizards also have long, forked tongues like that of a snake. They stick out their tongues and vibrate them rapidly. This behavior lets them detect the presence of potential prey. Like many reptiles, monitors have a specialized sense organ called the Jacobson's organ. It is sensitive to the smell of tiny particles that the lizard picks up from the air or ground with its forked tongue. The particles are transferred to the organ and the lizard can then trail its victim. This ability, halfway between taste and touch, is a true sixth sense.

The desert agama is an example of the chisel-teeth lizards, or agamids. This species is widespread from Morocco, along the northern edge of the Sahara, through the Arabian Desert, and as far as Iraq. It is not very colorful except during the mating period, when males turn luminous shades of blue.

The eyes of the agama lizard are protected by scaly eyelids, which extend like eyelashes to keep out sand.

During the day, agamas behave in ways that prevent sharp fluctuations in body temperature. In the morning they place themselves crosswise to the direction of the sun's rays so that they can absorb the largest possible amount of heat. In contrast, they expose the least possible body surface to the sun during the hottest hours and often keep their bellies lifted above the burning sand. The desert agama eats mainly orthopterons or other insects.

Another agama, the African spiny-tailed lizard, is a very unusual reptile of the great African desert. At one time, it was thought to be a vegetarian. Naturalists wondered how it could possibly survive during the dry season, when the grasses are only dry stems and green plants are scarce. Later it was discovered that this saurian generally eats crickets and grasshoppers, as well as beetles. From these insects, the lizard obtains some of the water needed to survive during the dry season.

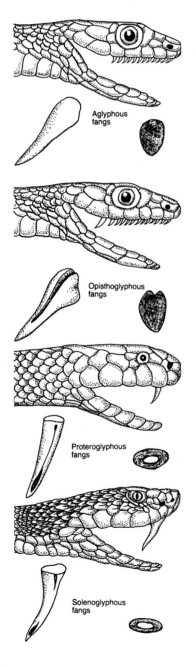

Illustrated are snake heads, fangs, and cross sections of fangs. Aglyphous fangs of harmless snakes are solid and do not carry venom. Opisthoglyphous venom fangs have a simple groove and are located in the back of the upper jaw. Proteroglyphous and solenoglyphous venom fangs are grooved, tubular, and located in the front part of the mouth. Solenoglyphous fangs are also movable.

Aglyphous fangs

Opisthoglyphous fangs

Proteroglyphous fangs

Solenoglyphous fangs

The spiny-tailed lizard has a large head covered with tough scales. Its rather stocky body varies in color from grayish brown to bright green. It has a unique tail that is layered with spiny scales to form a kind of armor. The tail is very wide, especially at the base, and almost as long as the lizard's entire body. The lizard hits possible predators with its tail to drive them away. At other times, the tail is used as a tool. The lizard also uses its tail to cover up the opening of its holes.

Snakes

Several snake species live in the desert areas of North Africa. In 1963, the German herpetologists (zoologists who study amphibians and reptiles) E. Kramer and H. Schnurrenberger listed seventeen species in Libya. In 1972, a French herpetologist, J. Bons, cited twenty-one species in Morocco. The most unusual snakes are sunbeam snakes, also known as "thread snakes." The heads and trunks of these slender snakes have the same diameter, making it difficult to tell one end from the other. Sunbeam snakes look blind because their eyes are hidden beneath the scales on the head. In fact, their Greek name means "the slender, blind ones." The same scales that are on the trunk also grow

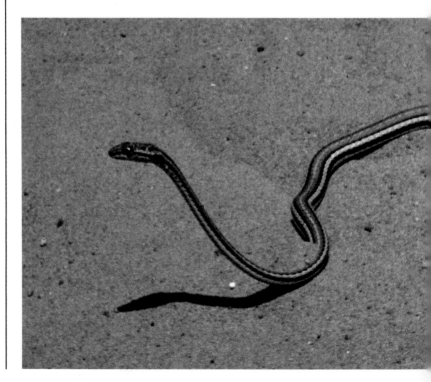

A sand-snake is a harmless, or colubrid, snake of arid regions. The thin and very long shape allows this snake to move quickly on the scalding ground. Surface contact is kept to a minimum to avoid overheating. Because its neck and head are so small, it can feed only on tiny prey.

on the tail. A cone-shaped shield, which sometimes has a spine, grows at the end of the tail.

The sunbeam snakes are the smallest known snakes. They are less than 6 inches (15 cm) long and 0.6 inches (1.5 cm) wide. Because of their small size, they could easily be mistaken for worms. They live secretive lives under the sand in the most arid areas. They come out at dusk to hunt the termites that are their main food source. These little reptiles are completely harmless to humans because their tiny mouths are too small to bite people.

Snakes are dangerous if they can inject venom when they bite. Those that inject venom have grooved fangs, which are connected to poison glands in the snake's upper jaw. Snakes are divided into four groups based on the type of fangs they have. First, there are the aglyphs. All the snakes in this group have solid fangs that do not carry poison to the victim. The opisthoglyphs have long, grooved fangs, which are the last or second-to-last fangs in the upper jaw. They are harmless to humans because the venomous back fangs cannot reach large prey. These fangs are also found in some non-venomous snakes. The proteroglyphs, an example of which is the cobra, have a pair of grooved fangs in the front of the upper jaw. They are dangerous to humans. Last, the

The horned viper is a common and very dangerous snake of the Saharan sands. Usually this snake lies buried in the sand. Only its eyes and devil-like horns show as it waits for prey. These poisonous reptiles are a deadly danger to small rodents and other small animals, as well as to unwary travelers who cross the sand without high, closed shoes.

solenoglyphs have fangs located in the front like the prote-roglyphs. However, these fangs are even more deadly. The snake can move them and turn them inward when biting. The viper is one snake that attacks this way. The most dangerous species belong to this last group.

A curious example of these unusual predators is the horned viper, which gets its name from the two horns on its head. Generally, it does not grow longer than about 24 inches (60 cm) and is a bleached yellow-gray or brown color.

The horned viper moves slowly, until it is ready to attack. Then it moves rapidly. During the day, it buries itself in the sand, leaving only its head showing. In this way, it blends into the environment and protects itself from enemies. At the same time, it protects itself from the sun. But if it is disturbed, the horned viper will swell up and hiss.

The horned viper leaves its own special tracks on the sand that make it easy to spot. The tracks appear as a series of dimples about 0.6 inches (1.5 cm) wide and 20 inches (.5 m) long. They form a ladder-like set of lines. The dimples are

Illustrated is the environment of the present day Bahariya oasis in Egypt as it probably appeared during the Mesozoic era (65 to 230 million years ago). Abundant vegetation grew on a vast plain near the sea, and large omnivorous (feeding on both plants and animals) reptiles lived there.

caused by the imprint of the vertebrae at the middle and below the tail. By following these dimples in the sand, a person could easily find the underground hiding place of the horned viper.

Reptiles of the Past

About 100 million years ago, a magnificent, humid palm forest existed where today there is desert. Many dinosaur species lived in this forest. Among these was the *aegyptosaurus*, a huge herbivore similar to the *brontosaurus*. *Dicraeosaurus* was another great herbivore that lived here. Some of these reptile species reached as much as 82 feet (25 m) in length.

Among the meat-eating animals, or carnivores, was the *spinosaurus*. It was about 40 feet (12 m) long and had a spiny fin on its back. This fin grew about 5 feet (1.5 m) out of the vertebrae. Other meat-eaters were the *Carcharodontosaurus*, which had sharpened, notched teeth like a shark; the *bahariasaurus*, one of the largest carnivores; and the *elaphrosaurus*, a small carnivore that could walk on two legs.

MAMMALS

Mammals and birds are warm-blooded animals that can regulate their internal body temperature. This ability gives them an advantage over reptiles, amphibians, and invertebrates which get most of their heat from their surroundings. Warm-blooded animals also have some clever ways of avoiding death from thirst or heat shock.

Rodents

Jerboas are perhaps the best known of the small desert mammals. They are found in the arid regions of North Africa, Arabia, and the Near East. The jerboa often can be seen standing erect on its long back legs or jumping like a miniature kangaroo. They have long tails that end in black-and-white tufts. Jerboas feed on plants, seeds, flowers, leaves, twigs from shrubs, and insects.

The hot desert sun presents a danger to the jerboa. The animal digs a deep burrow and uses it as a cool shelter during the day. In the burrow, the young are born and raised by the female. Researchers have measured the relative humidity inside these dens. It is between 30 and 50 percent, which is much higher than the 15 percent humidity of the outside air during the day. When adult jerboas leave their burrows at night to hunt, the relative humidity of the night air is almost the same as that inside the burrow.

Gerbils are another common mammal in North Africa. Though they resemble small rats, their thick, shiny hair gives them a more attractive appearance. They also have a kangaroo-like jump, but it is not as strong as the desert jerboa's.

The gerbil's burrow is a complex, underground maze. Above ground, it has a small, circular entrance. The gerbil closes this entrance during the heat of the day. The burrow is dug by the male and may cover several square yards of space. There are a number of underground tunnels, which are connected by passageways. In a special place, there is a nesting room for the females.

Herbivores

During periods of extreme drought, the intense heat and hungry locusts can completely destroy the scarce desert vegetation. Animals that eat only plant life have little chance of survival.

When vegetation is scarce, small rodents can live on insects. Other animals, such as gazelles and antelope, eat only plants. They are forced to migrate during the dry

Opposite page: An aoudad, or Barbary sheep, and its child are pictured. This beautiful ungulate, typical of the harshest and hottest deserts, is found today only in the least accessible places in the Sahara. All of the six known subspecies are considered endangered. These animals do exist in zoos throughout the world and breed well in captivity.

47

period each year to find food. The young adult males and females gather in large herds and search for other pastures. If these animals did not migrate each year, the scarce vegetation of desert and semidesert areas might be completely destroyed by overgrazing during the dry season.

The best known of the migratory herbivores is the dorcas gazelle. When the pastures start to dry up, the gazelles cross the western Sahara to the coast in search of food. Many of them, exhausted by hunger and thirst, die on the way. When the first rains fall and the grasses begin to grow, the surviving gazelles return to the interior regions.

Gazelles can live on a narrow diet. Their main food source is asfù. Gazelles eat asfù not only for its food value but also for the high water content of its succulent leaves. Gazelles also feed on various hard or spiny plant species such as acacias, rattlebox, and *Heliotrium*.

Females and young dorcas gazelles live in small groups. Adult males live alone, and each defends his own territory. Like many other ungulates, or hoofed animals, males visit the groups of females only during the mating period.

The desert gerbil is a common sight in arid lands. This rodent digs deep dens to take shelter from the sun and predators. Its diet consists mainly of plant matter. This food source provides the gerbil with the water it needs. Rodents inhabit different deserts of the world and have many qualities in common. Like the gerbil, they have many adaptations to help them survive in the desert.

48

Hoofed animals often have a system of signals to communicate with members of their own species. The dorcas gazelle and some species of deer make signal movements with the white areas of their backsides. The positions at the right give the following messages *(from top to bottom)*: calm, a flicking tail; slight alarm, the tail hanging down and the hindquarters lowered; strong alarm, the tail kept up high and the animal appearing tense.

These addaxes were photographed in a fenced area of the Hai Bar Reserve (Israel). This animal was once widespread in most of the Sahara. It was hunted to extinction in the desert, and today is not found north of the savannah region. The animals pictured are part of a special project in Israel. Naturalists there plan to reintroduce all large vertebrates that once existed in biblical times.

In the past, another species of gazelle, the dama gazelle, lived with the dorcas in the desert and semidesert regions. Herds with hundreds of gazelles formed all over the great desert to begin long migrations. The number of dorcas gazelles and another species, the edmi gazelle, has drastically decreased. Wealthy Europeans and a few land owners in the region became rich when oil was discovered on their land. They organized huge hunting parties and overhunted the gazelles for sport. After driving the unfortunate animals from their habitats, they chased them with cross-country vehicles. Sometimes they were armed with machine guns. In recent decades, other species of desert ungulates also have been slaughtered by this type of hunting. Today, the few remaining members of these species are forced to live in

the roughest, most remote areas where even four-wheel drive vehicles cannot go. Unfortunately, two of the five species of gazelles became extinct, and the remaining three are in danger of the same fate.

The scimitar-horned oryx was once widespread in all of the Sahara from west Africa to Egypt. Less than a century ago, this antelope was still abundant in southern Morocco and in parts of Algeria and Tunisia. Today, it lives only in southern Sahel, a small area south of its original home. Fortunately, this animal has been less persecuted than the Arabian oryx, which once could be found throughout the entire Arabian Peninsula including the Sinai and Mesopotamia. Now the Arabian oryx survives only in a semi-wild state in Jordan, Oman, and a few other protected locations where it has been introduced for breeding.

Another desert herbivore is the aoudad, or Barbary sheep. It looks like a cross between a goat and a sheep. Like a goat, its tail is short and hairless, and it has horns that form a triangle shape. The females have well-developed horns that grow to over 15 inches (40 cm). The horns of the adult male can reach over 30 inches (80 cm) in length. The Barbary sheep does not have the typical goat beard under the chin. However, between the throat and the chest of some males, there is a thick mane that grows down to the ground.

Barbary sheep are widespread in the rocky desert strip of North Africa. Six subspecies are known. All are threatened with extinction in the wild. Fortunately, this animal breeds well in zoos all over the world. Barbary sheep are nocturnal. They rest during the day and keep all activities to a minimum. During the night, they cross the rocky desert alone or in small groups, jumping and climbing with great ease. Barbary sheep graze in the morning or at dusk. They prefer tubers, which are the fleshy parts of plants that grow below the surface, like potatoes. They will also feed on grasses and dry shrubs.

Carnivores

Food in the desert is also scarce for carnivores, the animals that depend on meat for their food. These predators possess highly-developed sense organs that help them catch their prey.

Desert carnivores are examples of what ecologists call "Allen's Rule." Scientists observed that desert animals have larger legs, tails, and ears than similar species that live in cooler regions. They discovered that longer extremities help

The bodies of desert mammals show adaptations that set them apart from members of the same genus in temperate zones. The sand fox is much smaller than the European red fox and has much larger ears, which disperse more heat. The desert jerboa's legs and tail are much longer than those of the common wood mouse.

sand fox

European red fox

desert jerboa

wood mouse

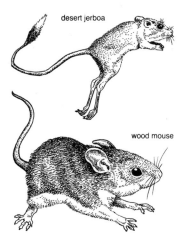

the animals get rid of excess heat.

The fennec illustrates Allen's Rule very well. The small Saharan fennec has ears much larger than its northern relatives, the European red fox and the arctic fox. Its body size also is a clue that it dwells in the Sahara. It weighs no more than about 3.5 pounds (1.5 kilograms). A red fox weighs from 11 to 14 pounds (5 to 6 kg) and, in northern Europe, can reach 24 pounds (11 kg).

The fennec has long, soft, cream-colored fur. On its back, the fur has reddish brown shadings. Around the eyes is a small, white mask with dark stripes. Its large ears, 6 inches (15 cm) or longer, are striped inside and edged with white fur. The fennec's very thick coat probably is there to protect these small desert foxes from low night temperatures during the Saharan winter.

Fennecs live in small groups of ten or fewer animals. They dig dens in the sand. These dens have a main room and several tunnels with exits. They spend the warm daytime hours in these underground homes. At night, the fennecs wander around the desert dunes. Their large ears are held high to pick up the sound of any prey that may lurk in the dark. They hunt and feed on insects, small reptiles, rodents, and small birds.

The sand fox is similar to both the fennec and the European red fox. Like the fennec, the sand fox's fur and tail are thick, but its ears are smaller. However, its ears are still larger than those of the European fox. The sand fox weighs 6 to 9 pounds (3 to 4 kg), which is heavier than the fennec.

Members of the dog family (canids) and those of the cat family (felids) range over the vast area from the Sahara to the deserts of the Arabian Peninsula and the land between the Caspian Sea and Pakistan. Among the cats, there have occurred some interesting adaptations to desert environments. One of the most beautiful and powerful cats is the caracal. It is found throughout the barren deserts and the arid lands of Africa.

Agile and powerful, the caracal was so admired for its hunting ability that the Persians and Indians trained it to hunt for them. As with its relative, the European lynx, the caracal has well-developed limbs, a small head, and a slender body. Its coat varies from dark red to grayish red or yellow-gray.

Caracals are active at dawn and dusk during the winter and at night during the summer. The long, sunny days are spent lying in the shelter of rocks or shrubs. They also are

A fennec has caught a mouse. The small desert fox feeds on rodents, reptiles, birds, and insects. Though it is the smallest member of the dog family in the Holarctic region, it is quite capable of taking care of itself. An Arab proverb says that the fennec "plays with two dogs, makes fun of three, relaxes when faced with four, flees if there are five, yet six dogs are needed to catch it."

found on the slopes of hills. There they find protection from the temperature and wind. The caracal is an expert bird hunter. It has great skill and patience. It stalks black-bellied and pintailed sand grouses in the morning as the flocks are about to fly off in search of water. Caracals often attack with a leap. They can catch their winged prey even if it is already 10 feet (3 m) into the air.

Another splendid cat is the cheetah, which was once present in the less arid regions of the Sahara. It now is very rare because of relentless trapping by Arabs who used it to hunt gazelles. This cat is much larger than the caracal. It differs from other members of its family because its claws do not retract, or draw back, when at rest. No other animal can match its speed on the ground. At full speed, it can run up to 70 miles (113 km) per hour. The swift gazelle can run 50 miles (80 km) per hour, and the fastest antelope can run 59 miles (95 km) per hour. However, they are no match for the cheetah and often fall as its prey.

BIRDS

The bodies of mammals, reptiles, and invertebrates have adaptations to help them deal with the heat and dryness of the desert. Birds have very few of these adaptations. In their form and appearance, they show little specialization for surviving in the desert. When the temperature reaches 122°F (50°C), birds will die. They can cool off slightly by keeping their bills open. In this position, water can evaporate from the mucous in the mouth. Panting releases some heat and slightly lowers the body temperature. Feathers also can aid in heat regulation. Birds keep their feathers tight and their wings slightly spread from the body so that air can circulate close to the body. When it is cold, the birds protect themselves by fluffing up their feathers.

Survival Strategies

Many bird species use several strategies to survive in the desert. The ability to fly plays an important role in these strategies. Some species make long daily flights in search of water. They rise high on air currents and descend in the heat only to search quickly for food. Some typical land species use the cooler hours of dawn and sunset to search for food and feed their chicks. When the sun is highest, they stay in the shade of a rock or stone. Land birds often are found near oases and where people have planted trees near roads and paths. Species like the cream-colored courser or the hoopoe lark can be observed standing with their bills open under the shade of young eucalyptus trees. Other species hide in dens. Small owls and common wheatears take over the abandoned dens of small mammals. Pale crag martins dig dens in the sandy walls of the *wadis* (dry riverbeds) and rest there during the hottest hours.

Granivorous birds feed mainly on seeds and grains, which are dry. For them, finding water to drink is a constant problem. Birds of prey and insectivorous birds have less of a need to find water because they get most of the water they need from the juicy animal tissues they eat. In general, birds need less water than mammals to eliminate wastes. Even the carnivorous birds, which have to get rid of excess nitrogen from the meat they eat, do not need as much water as mammals. They eliminate nitrogen as crystallized uric acid (the white part of their feces) rather than as urine.

Each day, granivorous birds make long flights for water because food and water are often far from each other. Sometimes, they even eat insects to get more water. Sparrows,

Opposite page: A black-bellied sand grouse is shown with its young. All species of sand grouse are land birds with coloring that blends into the environment. This adaptation is known as "cryptic coloration." Animals that dwell in the open desert tend to have paler upper bodies than those that spend the day in the shelter of bushes and vegetation.

55

Every day black-bellied sand grouse cover tens or hundreds of miles to reach safe waterholes. Besides drinking the water, sand grouse also soak their upper bodies so their chicks can get water from their wet feathers *(left).* This habit exposes sand grouse to the risk of predators. Birds of prey and carnivorous mammals have found that they can surprise the sand grouse as they drink because they do not lift their heads from the water *(center).* Some predators, like the lanner *(upper right),* attack the sand grouse as they are about to start on their long return trip.

larks, and calandra larks show this type of behavior.

Sand grouse are the most specialized birds in arid regions. They are similar to partridges, having strong wings, plump bodies, and short legs covered with feathers down to the toes. Species found in the Sahara are the black-bellied sand grouse, pintailed sand grouse, and Lichtenstein's sand grouse.

These birds nest in very dry areas where they are often the only birds to survive. They begin each day by gathering in large flocks and calling to each other with guttural cries. Then they fly to oases and waterholes that may be many miles away. Upon arrival, they drink even if the water is brackish, or salty. They are true experts at finding and using any precious water source available.

Sand grouse chicks do not feed on insects so they need a constant supply of water. Their water arrives in an original way. The adults drink at the distant waterholes. They lower the short, thick feathers of the neck and breast into the water. Sand grouse can drink this way because they have a special way of sucking in the liquid, like pigeons. They do

not have to lift their heads to swallow. After filling their feathers with water, the sand grouse fly back to the nesting site. The chicks get the water they need from these "living sponges" by passing the wet feathers through their beaks.

Black-bellied sand grouse exhibit another unusual adaptation. For protection from high temperatures, they have an air chamber between the thick skin of the abdomen and the connecting tissue, or fascia. This air chamber insulates the body from the heat. Because of this protection, the birds can stay on the ground under the sun even in the hottest hours. This thermal protection is used even by chicks that are only a few days old.

Cryptic Coloration

Many desert bird species have a cryptic coloration. In other words, they blend in with their surroundings, or camouflage themselves. This adaptation is useful to birds that spend most of their time on the ground. Such birds as houbara bustards, cream-colored coursers, larks, and many others prefer to walk on their strong legs rather than fly.

A cream-colored courser marches in the desert. This gull-like bird is different from most of the members of its order (Charadriiformes). It is found in somewhat humid areas and is a typical desert species. It seeks shade in the shelter of rocks or whatever vegetation may be available.

In a hot and dry environment, flying uses too much energy. Also, these birds may benefit from being on the ground because they are probably able to detect both predators and prey in the distance. Their prey are small reptiles and land arthropods, such as insects. In any case, if birds live in an area with almost no trees, they must learn to live on the ground.

The African houbara bustard is the largest among these ground-dwelling species. It is slightly more than 1.6 feet (.5 m) tall, with long, strong, greenish legs and a sandy back with gray streaks. Houbara bustards breed only if conditions are good. This special reproductive strategy is very useful in desert environments. If the season is too dry, they do not lay eggs at all. When conditions are good, they lay two or three in a depression in the ground.

Another species with cryptic coloration is the cream-colored courser. It is almost completely a sand color. Like the houbara bustard, it is widespread in the semidesert areas and stony deserts. Its strong, long legs are like those of its relatives, the shore-dwelling limicoline birds. This species, however, lives far from water. It feeds on land arthropods, which it hunts in the cooler hours of the day. When it is not breeding, this speedy, tireless runner travels distances

so great that they might be called migrations.

The stone curlew is a common species of arid regions. The sandy gray, streaked coloring of the curlew resembles the landscape. This type of camouflaging makes the bird hard to spot. Predators who look at the bird from the side are confused by the colors and cannot find it against the desert background. The pale coloration of its back feathers is from cells that produce pigments that are affected by high temperatures and low humidity. The breast and neck often have very bright coloration. These brighter colors are a way for other members of the same species to recognize one another. They are also used as a colorful signal during courtship displays. The same color pattern can act as a danger signal when one member of the flock suddenly takes flight.

Insectivorous Birds

Many birds that are granivorous do not eat only seeds and grains all year round. While breeding, or even in other seasons, some become insectivores.

One of these birds is the hoopoe lark, which inhabits all

The stone curlew is a gull-like bird found in arid, stony, or sandy regions. It is common in the semidesert areas of North Africa. It also inhabits the Iberian Peninsula and nests in many locations in central and eastern Europe during mild weather.

hoopoe lark

desert wheatear

pale crag martin

Desert birds have two ways to survive desert heat. They avoid contact with surfaces that are too hot, and they limit exposure to the sun's rays. The hoopoe lark builds its nest on a small bush to avoid the scorching soil temperature. The desert wheatear prefers a hole in the earth where it will be sheltered completely from the sun. The pale crag martin seeks out cavities in the walls of rocks for nesting and shelter during the hottest hours.

the desert areas of North Africa. It specializes in catching the adults and larvae of small beetles. It flushes these insects from the sand by digging with its long, down-curved bill. At first glance, this long-legged lark looks fairly ordinary. Its body is a pale camouflaging color with white and black bands on the flight feathers. But when it flies, the hoopoe lark is very colorful, like the magnificent hoopoe. During the breeding season, it chooses a low bush on which to build its nest. There it lays two to four eggs. It cannot build on the ground because the high temperatures would prevent the eggs from incubating. If they were born, the chicks could not survive the heat of the sand.

Other insectivorous desert birds are the cryptic-colored Tristram's warbler, and the desert wheatear, which has white upper-tail coverts (small feathers that grow at the base of larger ones), a black tail, darkish wings, and a general sandy tint. These land species can nest under a stone. Sometimes they can even be found nesting in the abandoned den of a small mammal. The cover protects the eggs and chicks from the sun.

Because of the desert's strong winds, there is little air-borne insect life. What there is of this food source is made up of tiny insects, beetles, and members of the orders Diptera (flies and mosquitoes) and Hymenoptera (wasps, ants, and bees). They swarm at a certain height above the ground. Because this source of food is scarce in the desert, swallows and common swifts, which live off air insects, are usually absent.

The pale crag martin uses special hunting techniques in these hostile environments. It seeks out wadis, gorges, and the small, sandy walls that are common in the desert. There are more winged insects in these spots because it is cooler. There is protection from the sun, and the wind is calmer. The crag martin's bill is stronger, and its wing surface is greater than related species. It can maneuver almost like a highly-skilled acrobat in the wind. Unlike other swallows, the pale crag martin catches and eats large, hard-shelled desert insects.

One of the most unusual insectivorous birds is the Egyptian nightjar. Its pale desert coloring makes it very difficult to detect. It is a very small bird, with a somewhat elongated shape and a short, wide bill. It hunts at dusk, using its long wings and tail to twist and turn in the air. The nightjar flies with its mouth wide open to gather insects swarming in small groups over the tops of bushes.

A desert lark on its nest is sheltered by a small plant tuft formed by a xerophyte (a plant adapted to living with a limited water supply). This little sand-colored bird is widespread in all of North Africa south of the nondesert strip along the Mediterranean. Compared to the other Saharan larks, this species has a shorter beak, and its feathers do not have contrasting colors.

Granivorous Birds

Some larks that live on the land have granivorous habits and, generally, camouflaging colors. Among these birds are the desert lark and the bar-tailed desert lark. Both are widespread in the Saharan areas. The most unusual of the desert larks is the thick-billed lark. This small land bird has a massive bill, and dark colors decorate parts of its body. A black spot marks each cheek, black bands are on the wings, and long black spots run along the breast and sides. Apart from those differences, the color is like that of most birds that blend into the background. It lays two to six raspberry-colored eggs, depending on the dryness of the year.

There are also some granivorous birds that migrate in search of food and water. Among them is the little trumpeter bullfinch, which is slightly smaller than a sparrow. It is known for its pale, rose feathers and for its song, which sounds like a toy trumpet. Trumpeter bullfinches live in desert and semidesert areas, where rocks, heaps of stones, and scattered shrubs dot the landscape. Outside of the nesting season, it is a rather gregarious bird that lives in small groups.

The Saharan desert sparrow also has desert coloring. It is the only sparrow that lives in the middle of the desert. This species is adapted to the sandy habitats and shrub-covered dunes of Morocco, Algeria, Tunisia, and Libya. It is not present in Egypt.

Winged Predators

The long journey of desert birds to and from the water holes may be as dangerous for them as for animals that travel overland. Fearsome predators patrol the skies. One such predator is the lanner falcon. The African lanner has a lighter back than its European relative. The upper part of the head is a beautiful yellow ocher, rather than red. It is about the same size as the peregrine falcon. The lanner uses a number of methods to catch insects, small mammals, and medium-sized birds. In general, the falcon takes flight from a rock, palm, or pole. A good glider finds an air current and rides it to 3,300 feet (1,000 m) or higher. At that height, the lanner stays cooler than if it were on the ground. It also can spot its prey from as far away as several miles. It is almost invisible from the ground because it flies so high and because of its white lower plumage. This coloration makes it very difficult to see from the ground. From high up, it chooses its prey and attacks with a speedy dive. Though the peregrine falcon's dive is faster, lanners are highly-skilled divers as well. Lanners may be observed hunting in pairs. One will frighten a group of birds on the ground, while the other captures one of them as they scatter. Using the same method, one of the birds will drive a small rodent from its hole, while the other waits to capture it.

In semidesert areas, the distribution of the lanner overlaps the area where the desert falcon lives. This species prefers a more rough and rocky habitat. It is so similar to the peregrine falcon that some authorities believe it is a subspecies. The desert falcon resembles a small lanner because of its small size and light-tinted back and yellowish nape (back of the neck). However, it chases its prey in the air like the peregrine falcon. A French ornithologist noted that the desert falcon and the lanner generally live in different habitats, and they fight fiercely when they meet.

Another bird of prey that is common in arid areas is a subspecies of the long-legged buzzard. It is not as strong a flier as the falcons and survives on insects, reptiles, and small mammals.

The nocturnal predators in the Sahara are camouflaged

Opposite page: Illustrated are some birds of prey that are typical of the Sahara. *Left to right, above:* the peregrine falcon and the lanner falcon; *middle:* the sooty falcon and the eagle owl; *below:* the little owl and the long-legged buzzard.

A stork nest on the ancient walls of the city of Marrakech in Morocco is pictured. The stork migrates in spring to North Africa and Europe where it spends the nesting season. In autumn, it goes to its winter home in the south-central part of Africa.

Opposite page: Shown are migratory routes of European storks. The migration of these large birds follows two main routes. One runs along the Strait of Gibraltar. The other crosses the Bosporus Strait as shown by the darker, wider lines on the map. The routes along the Channel of Sicily and the Peleponnesus, shown by the two lines in the center, are used less often. At some time, however, all European storks have to cross the Sahara Desert to reach their winter homes.

by light coloring. The most common are the great eagle owl and the little owl. Both are believed to be subspecies of European owls. They spend their days in ravines among the shelter of the rocks. At night they come out to catch mammals and, in the case of the little owl, small insects.

Migrations Between Europe and Africa

Many bird species that nest in the temperate areas of Europe and Asia migrate to tropical Africa during the colder seasons in the Northern Hemisphere. To reach the warm, abundant lands near the equator, they must cross large stretches of the Mediterranean Sea and the Sahara Desert without eating or drinking for long periods.

About 150 species of birds from the Palearctic spend the winter in groups of several hundred million in the

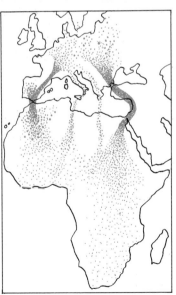

southern Sahara. These are estimates of R. E. Moreau, a noted scholar on migrations across the African continent. Numerous perching birds migrate across the Sahara. These migrating species include swallows, yellow wagtails, spotted flycatchers, warblers, blackcaps, common wheatears, golden orioles, and shrikes. Other migratory species are wrynecks (the only woodpecker to migrate long distances), Egyptian nightjars, common swifts, and quails. A number of birds of prey, such as honey buzzards and peregrine falcons, make the journey, as do aquatic birds of the Rallidae family (rails, crakes, and coots) and limicoline species.

Until about five thousand years ago, the western Sahara was covered with vegetation like that in temperate zones. Birds could stop for food and water as they flew through this region on their migrations. Now, they must travel over 900 miles (1,500 km) of desert where there is no food. Those that migrate long distances must have some adaptations to help them survive this difficult journey.

Some bird species make long migrations each year. They fly across the Sahara and often across a large part of Africa south of the desert, to nest in Europe. When winter comes to Europe, they return to the tropics. Biologists have been fascinated with the biology of these birds and have been puzzled by the behavior of young birds. The young can follow the migratory route even though they never made the journey before.

The German ornithologist Peter Berthold noticed that birds of the warbler family became very restless as the time of their usual migration neared. After a scientific study, Berthold found that birds that migrated long distances were uneasy for longer periods than those that migrated shorter distances. To measure the birds' restlessness, Berthold kept the birds in cages with perches that gave off electrical signals. Every time a bird touched the perching bar with its claws, the movement was registered on a roll of paper. Berthold conducted the experiment during a time when the birds would be getting ready to migrate if they were outdoors.

Berthold was able to show that Marmora's warbler, which migrates only 155 miles (250 km), has a relatively short period of pre-flight anxiety. On the other hand, the garden warbler, which migrates more than 3,000 miles (5,000 km), is restless much longer.

He concluded that birds know when to migrate because of an instinctive biological clock. Young birds only two or three months old can travel south alone. They decide on

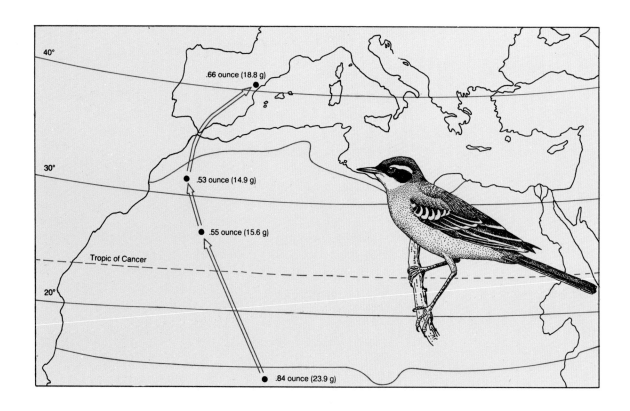

This diagram shows the yellow wagtail's energy consumption during its spring crossing of the Sahara. South of the desert (12 degrees latitude), its average weight is .84 ounce (23.9 g). By the time the bird reaches southern Algeria (27 degrees), its weight drops to .55 ounce (15.6 g). At the desert's northern border (32 degrees), it is only .53 ounce (14.9 g). When this endurance test is over, the bird's weight is regained rapidly. When it arrives in Spain (past 40 degrees), it already weighs .66 ounce (18.8 g).

their own when they will stop. To guide them during their very long trip, the birds use the sun, the stars, the earth's magnetic field, and probably other unknown factors. It seems certain that birds do not learn to navigate. They instinctively know because of heredity. The information is passed through the genes from generation to generation.

Long distance migrators show an increase in weight right before their journey. They build up fat stores because they will not have much food during the journey. In only ten days, they may increase their weight as much as 50 percent or more, depending on how far they will travel. An English ornithologist tells of an exhausted black wheatear that landed on a small boat about 310 miles (500 km) south of Iceland. The bird weighed about 0.75 ounce (21 grams). After six days of captivity and overeating, it was 1.25 ounces (35.5 g).

These birds show specialized behavior as well as specialized body functions. Just before migration, many diurnal bird species become restless and active during the night. This change in behavior prepares them for migration, most of which is done at night.

In 1982, an English ornithologist studied the loss of fat

Many migratory birds perish during the long trips, which are made twice a year through the desert. But many find safe resting places, where they stay for a short time before continuing their flight to their final destination. Pictured below is an exhausted house martin during its spring migration on the arid land of Cape Bon in northern Tunisia.

and the flight speed of migrating birds. He studied the yellow wagtail as it flew north during its nonstop journey across the Sahara. In northern Nigeria at twelve degrees north latitude, the weight of the birds was about .75 ounce (21 to 24 g). When they arrived in the Mediterranean at thirty-two degrees north latitude, it had dropped to .5 ounce (14 to 15 g), a loss of about 35 percent. According to Wood, the nonstop journey lasts sixty to seventy hours. During this difficult flight, birds suffer from water loss, but the major cause of death is exhaustion from flying against strong winds.

Fortunately, the yellow wagtail recovers rapidly. It quickly regains its fat deposits and its weight. Wagtails then keep the weight level up. At Camargue on the coast of France, wagtails were captured after crossing the Mediterranean. They had healthy weights. From other research, it has been shown that crossing the Sahara is more exhausting for the yellow wagtails than any other route they follow. After flying as far north as Lapland, they still weighed slightly more than .5 ounce (14 to 15 g), the same as what they weighed in the Mediterranean after recovering from crossing the desert.

OASES

The landscape of an oasis is mostly determined by people, but the survival of the plant life depends on the amount of water available in underground sources. People have planted date palms, which sink their roots deep into the ground to reach this moisture. The water of an oasis can come from a river, a spring, or the subsoil. In the last case, it is reached by digging artesian wells called *foggar*. The Nile River is also a great source of water. The larger oases are located along this river, and many people live near them.

The people of the Sahara cultivate the date palm in areas where water is available. They also produce tomatoes, onions, eggplants, peppers, carrots, watermelons, and other types of melon. In the oases, growers plant extensive citrus orchards and tropical vegetation. Farmers raise domestic and farmyard animals. For an arid region, there is a wide variety of agricultural activity.

Plants in the Sahara have always been a source of sustenance for people. Many trees and shrubs produce fruit that can be eaten. More grasslike species are used for their seeds or leaves. Still other species are pulpy and rich in starch. They are dried and made into flour. It can be used for animal fodder, for detergents, or for tanning hides.

Toxic substances like cyanic acid have been extracted from some plants. Certain Saharan leguminous plants and those of the Compositae family should not be eaten. A person's pulse rate will increase and eventually he or she will become very weak and may die. A well-known example of this harmful type of plant is *Hysosciamus falezlez,* which is a poisonous Old World herb. It contains powerful chemicals called "alkaloids." This plant is remembered for its use as a weapon by the Tuareg people to poison the members of the Flatters expedition in 1880.

Date Palm Cultivation

A main product of the desert oases is the fruit of the date palm tree. The best varieties are exported to Europe. Others are used as food for the desert dwellers. The *degla* palm tree produces one of the prized dates sold in Europe. It is known as *deglat-nour* meaning "fingers of light." This plant needs fresh water, but other trees can survive with poor quality water. For example, the palm that produces a lower quality date known as *ghar* can be grown where water is very salty. Ghar dates are dried in baskets and kept for several years. People in the region depend on these dates as an important food to keep in reserve.

Opposite page: This photograph was taken in springtime at the Nefta Oasis in Tunisia, where many tamarisks and date palms grow. Tens of thousands of palm and other fruit trees grow where water is available, and extensive areas have been irrigated.

69

Shown are date palms laden with fruit at a Saharan oasis. These trees probably are not native to North Africa. Today, however, they have become extremely important in the Sahara because the date is a very nutritious food. Many animal species depend on this fruit as the basis of their diets.

Date palms produce a fruit that is especially nourishing. People in the oases must be prepared to stand periods of scarcity. They have found that they can survive for a very long time by eating just milk and dates. This diet provides everything they need for their metabolism.

It is not easy, however, to grow healthy plants in the desert. This is especially true at the oases, where growers plant palms along ditches and canals. People continuously try to make the desert as green with vegetation as it once was centuries ago. At the same time, they struggle to maintain whatever fertile land they presently own. A *fellah,* or farmer, living at an oasis usually plants young palms in the sand and irrigates them twice a week when they are young. The roots soon grow in the direction of the water in the phreatic stratum (an underground level). Once their roots

The house bunting is as common in the desert villages as the sparrow is in the northern cities. It builds its nest in the cracks of walls or other openings in buildings. Occasionally, it may be found in isolated or high locations but never in the middle of the desert. Two subspecies are known throughout North Africa.

reach the water supply, the palms can survive alone. The fellah, however, will irrigate the plants when they produce fruit in order to obtain dates that are very pulpy.

The wind is the date grower's enemy. Because palms are planted in the more humid lowlands, they can be buried under the sand. The fellahs must continously remove the sand. They also try to block the blowing sand by putting up barriers of braided palm leaves.

Animal Life of the Oases

A person can estimate how fertile an oasis is by observing the number of animal species at the oasis. The little African green bee-eater is a common bird species at the oases. It is very small compared to similar species and is found only along the Nile. The Senegal coucal, a cuckoo, is found in the same areas. This large bird is black on its upper body. It is tinted bright green in spots. The wings are a brilliant chestnut color. Cuckoos have particularly interesting feet. They have toes that are different from most other species. Two toes point forward and two point backward, instead of three forward and one backward. Even more unusual is the long, thick nail in one of the two back toes. This species is active at dusk and, unlike many other cuckoos, does not take over the nests of other birds. It builds its own nest in which the female sits on the eggs.

Certainly the most common bird is the laughing dove. It can be seen wherever farmers are growing crops and near

Date palms grow in the Touggourt Oasis, Algeria. Growers are producing more of the prized deglat-nour date, which they export to Europe. They grow less of the older varieties, sometimes known as pasta dates, which are eaten by the local people.

A view from the Nile Valley in southern Egypt shows the river, vegetation, and, a short distance away, the desert. As it flows north, the Nile irrigates a narrow strip of land that winds like a long linear oasis from Sudan to the Mediterranean. This path of water and vegetation opens the way to many typically Ethiopian species of animals. They follow its course and travel far from the area where they usually live. In the past, the Nile and its fertile land drew even more species. Crocodiles, hippopotamuses, and sacred ibis once could be found in Egypt.

oases. Another species, the common bulbul, prefers palm groves. It can be recognized by its dark color and long tail. The song of the rufous bush robin is also part of desert life. This bird has a long tail that is pointed up. It is open like a fan to show off the black-and-white tip. One of the most trusting species is the house bunting, a perching bird with a grayish head and brownish body. This friendly bird is found wherever people make their homes at the oases, just as the house sparrow is found in the cities. A few years ago at a small settlement at an oasis in southern Tunisia, a pair of these birds was found nesting on the shelves of a grocery

store. They went in and out of the door window without any sign of fear.

The Nile Valley

The largest and most distinctive oasis inside the Sahara Desert is formed by the Nile Valley, which is at the eastern end of the Libyan-Egyptian desert. The source of the Nile River is Lake Victoria. It is found more than 4,000 miles (6,500 km) south of the city of Alexandria and the Mediterranean delta. In its very long journey to the north, the Nile first enters Sudan and flows west of the Ethiopian mountain range. Streams run down these mountains and pour into the Nile, swelling its size. The Nile then passes into land that becomes more and more parched. Here the river begins to evaporate quickly. The riverbed, however, is so huge and there are so many water sources flowing into it, that the Nile remains a powerful river. Unlike the wadis, it does not run dry before it reaches the sea.

As the branches of the Nile flow toward the Red Sea, they are stopped by mountains that rise to a height of 5,000 to 7,200 feet (1,500 to 2,200 m). These mountains run along the coast of northeast Africa, through southern Egypt, and on into the Arabian Desert in eastern Egypt. The Nile has not eroded new paths through the parched mountains. Instead, it continues north to the Mediterranean Sea and deposits its fertile silt around the coast. Egypt's unique and dramatic geography is clearly seen from the air. The Nile has tree-lined shores and is like a blue and green ribbon wandering through the middle of the land. On each side is the sandy, rocky desert, which appears grooved from the dried-up wadis. Among the huge areas of sand and rock, the river seems like something from another planet. It is an incredible sight.

In the time of Cheops and Chephren (kings and pyramid builders of Egypt), humans were already intensively exploiting this extraordinary land. Even so, vegetation and animal life thrived. Tall, elegant papyri grew in the water. Water lilies carpeted the calmer waters all the way from the Aswân waterfall in southern Egypt to the delta. Hippopotamuses and crocodiles lazily bathed, and large flocks of birds visited the river to search for food. Among these birds were the sacred ibis, Egyptian geese, ducks, cranes, herons, kites, vultures, and others.

Today, the Nile Valley appears completely covered with farms and other signs of agriculture. The land, however,

Shown are some of the most typical animal species that can be seen along the Egyptian Nile. *From left to right:* the caracal, the spur-winged plover, the dorcas gazelle, the pied kingfisher (flying and perching), the Nile monitor, the Egyptian goose, and Rüppell's vulture.

does not show obvious signs that people have exploited it. This is because most of the Egyptian people live in the major cities, and lush, tropical plants grow in the valley. The date palm, common banana, cotton, and sugarcane are common. To the visitor, the valley still appears to be an exotic paradise.

Not all the animals have been able to survive to this day. The sacred ibis, for example, has long since moved to land south of the Sahara. The hippopotamus disappeared from Egypt during the seventeenth century. A document from that time mentions that two of these large beasts were killed on July 20, 1600, on the delta near Damietta. The crocodile remained until about thirty years ago when the Aswân High Dam was built. Unfortunately, the dam blocked the crocodile's way to the river north of Lake Nasser. Another great reptile, the Nile monitor lizard, has survived and can be found along the entire length of the river. Up to 6.6 feet (2 m) long, the monitor depends on water to survive.

The Nile monitor is a powerful swimmer and uses its strong tail to guide it through the water. Unlike its relative, the desert monitor, this species's tail is very flat. When frightened, it usually heads for the water.

Some of the most spectacularly colorful birds in North Africa live in the Nile Valley. Besides the usual species found at the oases, such as the laughing dove, the common bulbul, and the hoopoe, there are many aquatic birds. Included are the cattle egret, the spur-winged plover, and the Egyptian goose. In the winter, many other species of ducks can be seen. The visiting ducks include teals, garganeys, wigeons, pintails, shovelers, tufted ducks, pochards, ruddy shelducks, greylag geese, and white-fronted geese. The red-breasted goose migrates from distant Siberia to winter in this valley, though only a few are now sighted. Long ago it must have been common because it is depicted in a famous painting from the Egyptian tomb of Itet, which was built in 2,500 B.C.

THE MOROCCAN ATLAS MOUNTAINS

The Atlas Mountain chain, with peaks that reach heights of 13,000 feet (4,000 m) or more, form the backbone of the region known as the Maghreb (Morocco, Algeria, and Tunisia). The Greek historian Herodotus named the mountains in honor of Atlas, the mythical god who held up the heavens. The Atlas Mountains are part of a ring of mountain ranges that form a circle around the western basin of the Mediterranean. To the west, the Atlas links up with the Spanish Penibetico Mountains. These eventually connect with the Italian Apennines. In a geological sense, these mountains are young.

The Atlas Mountains are formed by two chains, one in the interior and the other near the coast. Plateaus, such as the Meseta in Morocco and others in Algeria, lie between the chains. The Rif Atlas Mountains along the coast in Morocco reach 8,200 feet (2,500 m) in height. The rough, steep mountain slopes descend directly to the sea at some places. The inland chain is formed by the limestone-based Middle Atlas Mountains. They are lower and resemble a series of lengthwise ridges. In Algeria, the Saharan Atlas Mountains form a barrier between the desert regions and the Mediterranean. South of the Middle Atlas is the High Atlas. This chain extends for about 435 miles (700 km) southeast of Marrakech, in Morocco. The highest peak of this lofty mountain chain is Toubkal. This Alpine-like peak rises to 13,665 feet (4,165 m) and is snow-covered most of the year, until late spring or the beginning of summer. The eastern part of the chain is a series of rather unspectacular mountains also called the High Atlas.

The Climate

The Atlas Mountains are in a temperate zone with a Mediterranean climate. Rain falls mainly during the cold months, and summer is very hot and dry. The distance from the Atlantic Ocean and the altitude are two factors that influence the climate of these mountains. In the mountains far from the sea, the low temperatures drop lower and the high temperatures rise higher than in those areas closer to the sea. In other words, the temperature range is more extreme. This means that at the higher altitudes, the temperatures are cooler in the warm season and colder in the winter.

The average low temperature in the coldest months is below 50°F (10°C), but inland it goes down to less than 32°F (0°C) in the highest places. During the hottest months, the

Opposite page: Pictured is the majestic Toubkal Mountain in the Moroccan High Atlas. It is 13,665 feet (4,165 m) high and snow covered most of the year. This imposing mountain is not only the highest peak of the Atlas, it is also one of the most spectacular natural phenomena in all of North Africa.

79

A cedar forest at Azrou in the Middle Atlas Mountains is shown. These typical native plant formations reach their full growth in the humid Mediterranean vegetation strip. Deciduous oaks grow here at the lower altitudes, and cedar forests grow at higher altitudes. The undergrowth includes both Mediterranean plants and deciduous forest shrubs.

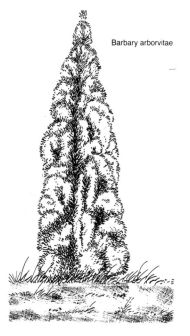

Barbary arborvitae

average high temperature is about 86°F (30°C) along the Atlantic coast and in the high mountains. During those months in the central plateau, the temperature is higher, 91.4°F (33°C). The amount of precipitation varies from year to year. The usual rainy or snowy times are at the end of autumn and the end of winter.

During the winter, snow is common at altitudes of 3,280 feet (1,000 m) and higher. The snow melts quickly except in the high areas where the temperatures are very cold.

Vegetation

In general, there are six climatic zones: Saharan, arid, semiarid, sub-humid, humid, and high mountain. In each zone, a particular kind of plant life is found. The phrase "climatic strip of vegetation" refers to the type of plant life particular to a climatic zone.

The semiarid Mediterranean strip of vegetation is

Atlas cedar

characterized by cork plantations, ilex groves, and oriental arborvitae (evergreen) forests. Each species can be found where landscape and local climate are suitable for it.

The Barbary arborvitae, a species endemic to North Africa, thrives in a semiarid Mediterranean climate with cool or temperate winters. Arborvitae forests in Morocco cover a surface of 2,567 sq. miles (6,650 sq. km). The final, stable stage of a plant community, the climax stage, is made up of small forests with mastic, wild olive, phillyrea, lavender, and cistus.

Cork oak is a calcifuge tree. This means it does not need calcium-rich soil to grow. It is found in Morocco in semi-arid, sub-humid, and humid zones. Cork plantations cover a total surface of 1,544 sq. miles (4,000 sq. km) below 2,625 feet (800 m) in altitude. The plantations have an undergrowth of strawberry tree, broom tree, and cistus. The grassy layers include wild marjoram and milk vetch.

Holm oak is found between semiarid and humid regions and is common in Morocco. It covers a total surface of 2,702 sq. miles (7,000 sq. km). This tree is able to survive in a remarkable variety of environments. It is found from about 1,000 to 9,500 feet (300 to 2,900 m) in the High Atlas. In the Middle Atlas, its range is more limited. Holm oak disappears along the Atlantic coast, where it is replaced by cork oak and oriental arborvitae.

The sub-humid Mediterranean coastal region consists essentially of cork oak or holm oak. Pinaster also appears there as well as zeen oak and the Atlas cedar. These three species grow to maturity only in the humid strip of land along the sea.

In the sub-humid areas of the Atlas Mountains, cork plantations are so numerous that they create a green dome overhead. Beneath them is a rich undergrowth of holm oak, broom, four-flowered broom, strawberry tree, and various cistuses. There are also sub-humid holm oak groves, which are low, very dense forests. The underbrush is not very abundant. These oaks are quite rare and almost all are somewhat underdeveloped.

The humid Mediterranean climate has high rainfall and a short, dry summer. Deciduous oaks and cedars grow in this humid strip where the soil is rich. Here the holm oak forests are different from those present in other vegetational strips. The trees can reach 66 feet (20 m) in height. The underbrush is very dense and includes strawberry trees, viburnum, running swamp blackberry, English holly, and cistus.

Oaks, such as the zeen oak, grow on the humid strip and cover about 93 sq. miles (240 sq. km) of Morocco. They form a dense forest reaching 98 feet (30 m) in height. Immediately below the oak zone are the low cedars. They are found in mixed forests in the intermediate zones. Or they exist as the only mature tree in pure forests where holm oak is reduced to undergrowth.

Moroccan pinaster can be found from 5,570 to 6,070 feet (1,700 to 1,850 m) above sea level. Great, pure pinaster forests are found on dolomite, which is sedimentary rock made of calcium magnesium carbonate. The underbrush is holm oak, English hawthorn, and viburnum.

The Fauna of the Atlas Mountains

The Atlas Mountains are populated by an interesting variety of animal life. In ancient times, many of these ani-

Opposite page: Atlas cedars appear on the Rif Mountain range. The word *cedar* comes from the ancient Greek name *kedros.*

Pictured is a Barbary ground squirrel. Typically terrestrial, these squirrels are closely related to the ground squirrels of East Africa.

mals came to this area by two main routes. Some moved south through Europe and across the Iberian Peninsula. Others came north from central Africa across the Sahara. At that time, the desert was not as dry and inhospitable as it is today.

Typical European animals such as the brown bear, red deer, and red fox appeared in the Atlas Mountains. Other species were Ethiopian, such as the lion, leopard, striped hyena, honey badger, and the helmeted guineafowl. Endemic species were also present. Some of these were the Barbary ape, the Barbary ground squirrel, and many reptiles. Although the lion, bear, and Barbary deer are now extinct in Morocco because of attacks by humans, there still are many fascinating animals in the area.

One of the most interesting is the honey badger. The appearance and behavior of this robust carnivore somewhat resembles the Old World badger. The Barbary ground squirrel is related to the African ground squirrels of the savannahs, south of the Sahara. Like its relatives, this squirrel digs complicated tunnels in the ground. There it stores seeds, bulbs, and fruit for the winter.

Of the birds, the bald ibis is undoubtedly the most exotic. It is an unusual member of the Ciconiiformes order,

The bald ibis is one of the rarest and most endangered birds of its family. The causes for its decline are not well known because it is not hunted by humans nor has its habitat been destroyed. Because the few remaining wild populations are endangered, some zoos are breeding them in captivity.

which includes herons, the hammerhead, storks, the shoe-bill, ibises, and spoonbills. The bald ibis measures between 28 and 30 inches (70 to 75 cm) long and resembles the glossy ibis. Its head is naked, except for hairy, lance-like feathers. Until the seventeenth century, this bird nested in Switzerland and other spots in central Europe. Today, most of the surviving populations are in Morocco.

By the end of the First World War, one colony of several hundred pairs remained in the Near East at Birecik, Turkey. Today, only a few pairs survive there. There is a colony of about ten pairs in Algeria, between Boukhari and Bougzoul. This colony was discovered a century and a half ago, and it survived until 1940. The colony appeared to be very productive. Each female regularly laid five to six eggs in a nest. Nonetheless, the colony almost has disappeared today. In Morocco, it lives between the Mediterranean coast and the Tekna region. Naturalists estimated the total population at 600 to 650 ibis in 1977.

THE CANARY, MADEIRA, AND AZORES ISLANDS

In the Atlantic Ocean off the northwestern African coast, are three archipelagoes or groups of islands. These three island groups are the Canary, Madeira, and Azores. Even though they are rather far apart, they all have similar climates and are covered by lush vegetation. Some of the Sahara's dry conditions exist on the Canary Islands. As one moves northwest beyond the Canaries to the Madeira Islands, the arid climate becomes more temperate. It is even milder in the farthest group, the Azores. Animal and plant species that originated in different climates are found living together on these islands. For example, species that are characteristic of European forests are found growing near typical Saharan species.

These islands are particularly interesting places to study because of their insularity, or being shut off from the influences of other lands. Many endemic species are found on these archipelagoes. These unique types fascinate scientists who study the evolution of plants and animals on islands.

The Azores

The Azores is a wild archipelago of volcanic origin. It lies 870 miles (1,400 km) from Europe and 2,485 miles (4,000 km) from America. In 1432, the Portuguese came to colonize the island and sighted some birds of prey flying over. Thinking they were goshawks, or *acors* in Portuguese, they named the island after them. The Azores had probably been visited earlier by navigators from Carthage, an ancient city near what is now Tunisia. Today, the Azores are covered mostly by banana plantations, vineyards, citrus orchards, tea plantations, tobacco, pineapple (in greenhouses), and sweet potatoes. Several plant species of natural origin still flower there.

The total surface area of the archipelago's nine islands is 895 sq. miles (2,324 sq. km). From east to west, they are: Santa Maria, 37 sq. miles (97 sq. km); São Miguel, 288 sq. miles (747 sq. km): Terceira, 153 sq. miles (397 sq. km); Graciosa, 31 sq. miles (80 sq. km); São Jorge, 92 sq. miles (238 sq. km); Pico, 167 sq. miles (433 sq. km); Faial, 66 sq. miles (172 sq. km); Corvo, 6.5 sq. miles (17 sq. km); and Flores, 55 sq. miles (143 sq. km).

On São Miguel, one of the larger islands, hot springs support lush tropical vegetation. There are two small lakes in the crater of Caldeira. Santa Maria is the only island with traces of calcium carbonate, a white, crystalline mineral

Opposite page: The origin of the Azores is ancient volcanic activity, the scars of which still can be seen on the island landscape. Pictured is an extinct crater on the island of São Miguel, which is the largest in the archipelago.

THE AZORES

Corvo
Flores
Graciosa
Faial
São Jorge
Terceira Pico
Pico
São Miguel
Santa Maria

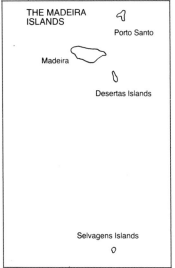

THE MADEIRA ISLANDS

Porto Santo
Madeira
Desertas Islands
Selvagens Islands

THE CANARY ISLANDS

Lanzarote
La Palma
Tenerife
Gomera
Fuerteventura
Grand Canary
AFRICA

Pictured are maps showing the Azores, Madeira, and the Canary islands. Those islands that have had recent volcanic activity are shaded. The three archipelagoes generally have similar climatic conditions and vegetation. They are all of volcanic origin.

found in rocks. On this island, these rocks are found among the massive volcanic formations. Graciosa is drier and barely reaches 1,312 feet (400 m) above sea level. There is an active volcano on this island. It contains a small lake with sulfurous water. The lake can be reached by a long, spiral staircase. São Jorge is the most famous island because of the hydrangeas, flowering shrubs that cover the area with their multicolored vegetation.

Faial has the greatest volcanic activity, and Pico is the tallest island, rising 7,612 feet (2,320 m) high. Its peaks are often covered in fog or snow. Flores is at the westernmost point of the group and is, perhaps, the wildest. Corvo is the smallest. There are two small lakes, separated by two islets, at a depth of 984 feet (300 m) in its crater. On the whole, the climate of the Azores is mild. The average temperature is 57°F (14°C) in January and 71°F (22°C) in August. Annual rainfall is 35 inches (900 mm). The climate is further tempered by the Gulf Stream.

The volcanic activity that created the Azores has not ended. Minor eruptions occur from time to time. Some catastrophic, tragic earthquakes still occur. The most recent was on the island of Terceira in 1980. In 1957, a powerful quake shook Faial. The island sank 1.6 feet (.5 m) and widened .15 sq. miles (.38 sq. km) on one slope. A museum featuring the history of the volcano was established after the 1957 eruption.

Herman Melville, the author of *Moby Dick,* wrote that the best whalers were from the Azores. Their trophies, utensils, objects of carved bone, documents, and books on whaling are gathered today in the Lajes do Pico whale museum. The museum tells the story of the ancient profession that has today almost totally died out. The decrease in the whale population is not the reason that whaling has declined. The real reasons are because there is less demand for whale oil, and people prefer less difficult work.

The Madeira Islands

Created from volcanic eruptions , the Madeira Islands are located 338 miles (545 km) northwest of the African coast and cover an area of 308 sq. miles (797 sq. km). They consist of two large islands, Madeira and Porto Santo, and smaller groups, including the Desertas and the Selvagens Islands. First discovered in ancient times, they were colonized by the Portuguese in 1420. The islands of the Madeira archipelago were formed by a succession of underwater

A strelitzia, or bird-of-paradise flower, grows in a garden on Madeira. Native to South Africa, this bushy plant is a perennial. It thrives in Mediterranean subtropical climates. In Europe, it is cultivated in the ground or in vases.

volcanoes, which caused the rugged appearance of the islands and their deep valleys. The tallest peak in Madeira is Pico Ruivo de Santa Ana at 6,060 feet (1,847 m). The Deserta Islands rise along this mountain chain. The climate of this archipelago is mild, with an average temperature of 66°F (19°C). February temperatures are about 59°F (15°C), and August is warmer at 71°F (22°C). Rainfall is never greater than 23.6 inches (600 mm) per year.

The Selvagens and Desertas Islands are located 146 miles (235 km) south of Madeira, 99 miles (160 km) north of Tenerife (Canaries), and 373 miles (600 km) west of Cape

Shown is a landscape on Grand Canary with a group of agaves (plants introduced from Central America) in the foreground. In the background is the island of Tenerife with its peak, Teide, rising to 12,192 feet (3,716 m). Among the Atlantic islands off the African coasts, the Canaries have climatic conditions closest to those in the Sahara.

Rhir in Morocco. The archipelago is formed by three main uninhabited islands. The largest is Selvagen Grande and the smaller are Pitao Grande and Pitao Pequeño. They are volcanic islands and have halophilic vegetation, which means "thriving in salty soil."

Selvagen Grañde occupies only about 1 sq. mile (2.5 sq. km) and barely tops 502 feet (153 m) in height. Its sheer cliffs jut out at some points to 295 feet (90 m), making it hard to climb. This tiny archipelago is most famous among naturalists for its bird colonies. These colonies contain several thousand pairs of Cory's shearwaters and Bulwer's petrels. Unfortunately, local fishermen capture the chicks for food, and survival of these marine birds is threatened.

The Canary Islands

The Canary Islands have been known since the time of the Phoenicians, about the fourth century B.C. They were colonized in 1300 by Lanzarotto Malocello, a navigator from Genoa, Italy. Lanzarote Island bears his name. The Canaries have a total surface area of 2,807 sq. miles (7,273 sq. km), widespread over seven larger islands and some tiny reefs.

They are volcanically formed islands and are linked to the Atlas Mountain system. Geologically, these are old islands. It is believed that the Canaries appeared at the same time that the continent of Atlantis was formed, about 600 to 100 million years ago. Atlantis was located off the Strait of Gibraltar in the Atlantic Ocean. Only the Canaries, Azores, and Greenland are left from this immense continent which gradually became submerged.

From east to west, the islands that make up the Canaries are Lanzarote, Fuerteventura, Grand Canary, Tenerife, Gomera, La Palma, and Hierro. Recent volcanic activity has been found only on Lanzarote, Tenerife, and La Palma. The summit is Pico de Teide on Tenerife which rises to 12,192 feet (3,716 m). The climate is mild, with small annual temperature variations. Tenerife averages 62°F (16.7°C) and La Palma, 68°F (20°C). The summer heat is tempered by the sea breezes, while the winter is warmed by the Saharan winds.

Much of the plant life of the Canary Islands is found in Mediterranean lands as well. Some species characteristic of the Cape Verde, Canary, Madeira, and Azores islands can also be found in Morocco. Other species that are found on the continent do not appear on the islands.

The studies of Braun-Blanquet and Maire suggest that the southern coast of Morocco and the Canaries were connected between 2 and 65 million years ago, during the Tertiary period. This link may explain the similarities in plants and animals found on these two land masses. In fact, some species that inhabit the Canaries today can be considered relicts, which are plant or animal survivors of an earlier era. Relatives of these old survivors can be found far apart. For example, a common species in the Canaries and Morocco is *Drusa oppositifolia*, a member of the Umbelliferae or parsley family. Related species exist as far away as America. This fact suggests that it is a relict from the time the African and American continents were joined. Some Canarian species are also present in South America.

The Canaries have many endemic species. A total of 469 have been identified on the Canaries, Madeira, and Azores.

The four most western islands—Hierro, La Palma, Gomera, and Tenerife—look remarkably green because of the Passat cloud. This cloud generally brings high humidity but no rain. The moisture in the air condenses on the plants' leaves at altitudes from 1,640 to 4,921 feet (500 to 1,500 m) and sometimes at heights of 7,546 feet (2,300 m).

According to studies, the Canaries have three distinct vegetation zones. The lowest is the sea vegetation strip which reaches an altitude of 1,969 feet (600 m). Mostly tropical vegetation grows here. Some rare forests are found at altitudes of 1,312 to 1,640 feet (400 to 500 m) high on La Palma and Tenerife. The plants of this strip include all the rock, sea, and cliff species, as well as those living on the sandy coast and low-lying plains. Among the endemic varieties are several shrubby plants of the Crassulaceae, or orpine, family and the Canary Islands date palm.

Many large green plants that are used as house plants in northern climates grow naturally here. However, they grow much larger on the islands, reaching the size of trees. One of them is the dracaena. Dracaenas are very long-lived, and the Canary dracaena produces a gum resin known as "Canarian dragon's blood." Another dracaena, the dragon tree, is a fairly well-known plant that can be found on Madeira and the Cape Verde Islands. It has been exported everywhere as an ornamental plant. Today, this large dracaena reproduces naturally only on Tenerife and La Palma. Canarian spurges can be found in the sea strip up to 984 feet (300 m) high. They are similar to some cacti and are quite

Opposite page: Illustrated are the strips of vegetation recognizable on the Canary Islands. *Bottom:* Up to about 1,970 feet (600 m) in altitude, there are subtropical cultivations. Forests, which are now rare, include such plants as *(from left to right)* alm, dracaena, broom, and spurges. *Middle:* Between 1,970 and 5,900 feet (600 to 1,800 m) high, there are forests of endemic pine *(left)* and laurel *(right)* species. *Top:* Above 5,900 feet (1,800 m), grow mostly xerophytes such as heather and thyme.

The common Canary Island lizard, the most widespread lizard on the Canaries, can reach a total length of about 20 inches (50 cm). A number of subspecies, which vary greatly in color, live on the different islands of the archipelago. The common lizard's back is generally greenish and speckled. It displays a variable number of sky blue patches and eyespots.

common in the hot, dry, rocky habitats of the central islands.

The second distinct plant zone is the woodlands. They are found at altitudes between 1,969 and 5,906 feet (600 to 1,800 m). These forests contain laurel and pine species that are endemic to the Canaries. Unfortunately, because of coal mining, the lumber industry, and agriculture, most of the once splendid and well-developed laurel forests have been destroyed. Today, they exist only on the islands where the highlands exceed 1,969 feet (600 m). The light penetrates dimly for only a few hours every day in these dense forests. Beneath the trees is a thick layer of humus that has built up from the large amount of decaying plant material. Many springs feed this fertile land, giving many species of ferns a favorable place to grow. Of all the endemic plants in the woodland strip, the most interesting are the species of laurel and one type of strawberry tree.

The third strip is the upper woodland and subalpine zone, found above 5,906 feet (1,800 m). In these colder temperatures, the vegetation is sparse because snow slows its growth. Mostly xerophytes grow here, many of which are endemic and show special adaptations.

The careful observer visiting Tenerife or one of the other three western islands has an excellent chance of sighting the common Canary Island lizard. Usually it can be found motionless on the rocks, ready to defend its territory.

On the various islands of the Canarian archipelago, the number of bird species depends more on the altitude (and, therefore, the variety of habitats) than on the distance from the African coast or the surface area of the island. For example, on Tenerife, there are thirty-five bird species, but on Fuerteventura (which is only a little smaller and much closer to the African coast), there are nineteen. Tenerife reaches a height of 12,192 feet (3,716 m), compared to Fuerteventura's 2,648 feet (807 m).

This lizard grows to 1.6 feet (.5 m) long, and its dorsal scales vary in color depending on which of the four islands it inhabits. On Tenerife, the lizard shows a greenish design with dark strips crossing its back. On La Palma, it has a bright blue head and cheeks and an even-toned body.

On Gomera, the lizard's color is very dark. On Hierro, the lizard has become dwarfed. These lizards feed on plants, seeds, and fleshy fruit, from which they obtain water. Occasionally, they are known to eat small invertebrates.

The purpurian lizard is common only on the most eastern islands and endemic to the Canaries. Barely reaching 10 inches (25 cm) long, it resembles the species mentioned above. A third species that lives on Grand Canary is Stehlin's lizard, a large saurian that sometimes grows longer than 23.6 inches (60 cm). Locally, this species is called *lagartos*. When excited, this large lizard will make the same short, strident cries for which the other Canarian species are known. The Simony's lizard was a fourth variety. It lived on

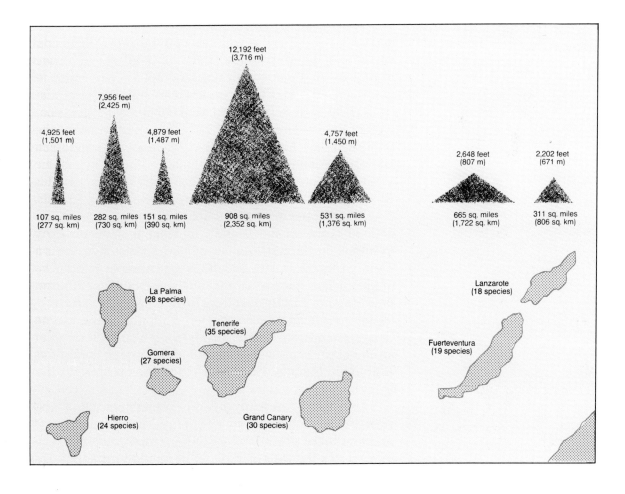

canarian oystercatcher

Rufous bush robin

chaffinch

chough

the tiny reefs off the island of Hierro. Similar in size and type to the Stehlin's lizard, it became extinct in the 1940s. This extinction probably happened because of both natural and human causes.

Natural Laboratories for the Ecologist

"It is an extraordinary experience for the European bird-watcher to walk through the broad-leaved forests on Tenerife," wrote the English ornithologist David Lack in his book *Island Biology*. The birds on this island are unusual for several reasons. First, there are many endemic species. Second, many birds show special adaptations or, as a naturalist might say, they fill unusual ecological niches. There are great numbers of birds to see, even though they represent a small number of species. In the forests of Tenerife, there are only ten species of birds that nest on land. A total of 34 such species live on all the Canaries. In comparison with this amount, 130 species are known to nest on the mainland in Morocco.

The ornithologists Lack and Southern were among the first to discover that the Atlantic islands were an ecological and biogeographic treasure. (*Biographic* refers to a branch of biology that deals with the geographic distribution of plants and animals.) They came to learn how island species were affected by being cut off from contact with species on the continent. They studied the effects of insularity and published their findings in 1949. This report was an important source of new information. Lack continued to be interested in this problem, and there are many references to the Atlantic islands in his later writings.

The number of species that lives on an island seems to depend more on the island's location than its size. For example, the largest number of bird species lives on the Canary Islands, and the second largest number is found on Madeira. The Azores, as previously mentioned, are larger than Madeira. Madeira is closer to the continent, which may be the reason that more species are found there. On the Canary Islands, the number of land birds also depends more on the altitude of each island than its surface conditions. Altitude influences the type of vegetation and insects that will grow in a certain area.

Land that offers many different habitats also has a large variety of food choices for birds. Many different species will seek out these places to satisfy their food preferences. In other words, the variety of available habitats influences the

The rock sparrow was originally the only representative of its family on the Canary Islands. In the absence of competitors, it lived in cities just like the house sparrow. After the arrival of the Spanish sparrow in 1850, the rock sparrow retired to the countryside. Today, it is found mainly in rocky habitats.

number of species present. Therefore, the fewer number of species on the Azores is a result of their greater isolation and because the islands have fewer types of habitats. In fact, Lack found that some species that live on the Canary Islands are not able to find the habitats they need on Madeira or the Azores. Lack's research did not have all the answers, however. It may be chance that some species never appear in certain locations, or competition with other species may drive some off.

The chough is one bird species that puzzles naturalists. This member of the crow family is black, with red legs and bill. It is an everyday sight on the island of La Palma in both wild and cultivated areas. This species, however, is absent from the rest of the Canarian archipelago. Distance is not an obstacle because the bird could fly from La Palma to one of the other islands within an hour. Attempts to introduce it on Tenerife have been unsuccessful.

There are few migratory species on the islands. Perhaps they cannot compete with the species that already inhabit the land. It seems logical that a species that is already

Canarian laurel pigeon

long-toed pigeon

plain swift

well established and has adapted slowly to special environments would have an advantage over newcomers. It is not always so. Some species, however, are successful at quickly adapting to new places and may displace native species. One example is the common sparrow. Originally, only the rock sparrow was widespread in the fields and cities of the central and western Canary Islands. In 1850, the Spanish sparrow arrived on Grand Canary Island. This species was common in Morocco, Spain, and most of the Mediterranean. When the Spanish sparrow moved in, the rock sparrow left the cities and could be found only in the countryside. The two species separated and began to occupy different ecological niches, where they did not interfere with each other. This situation was repeated on Madeira.

Some species of birds share the space on islands. By doing so, they have less room and fewer food sources per individual. Other species enlarge their niche when there are no others around to compete with them. The chaffinch is an example of a species that limits its niche when sharing space and resources. Particular birds known as blue tits expand their niche when competition from other species is low.

Two species have disappeared from the Canary Islands in the last few years. The red kite, a large bird of prey, was so abundant on Tenerife, Gomera, Hierro, and Grand Canary in the 1920s that it was considered to be the most common bird of prey. It became extinct because of DDT and other insecticides, which were used in the fight against locusts.

The Canarian oystercatcher, a close relative of a South African species, used to breed on Fuerteventura, Lanzarote, and the reefs of Alegranza, Lobos, Montaña Clara, and Graciosa. It fed on bivalve mollusks. There have been no reports of this species since the 1960s. It is probably extinct, though the cause is unknown.

Endemic Birds of the Atlantic Islands

There are a total of seven endemic species of birds on the Azores, Madeira, and the Canaries. The largest number is on the Canary Islands. They show the most unusual adaptations.

Canarian laurel pigeon. Almost as large as a woodpigeon, this species has gray-chestnut coloring. It lives in laurel forests and rocky areas of La Palma, Gomera, and Tenerife. According to the latest ornithological observations, it is still a common species.

Canarian pipit

Canarian chat

Teydean chaffinch

Long-toed pigeon. This species is dark gray above a reddish breast and is about the size of the woodpigeon. It also lives in laurel forests, where it feeds on berries. It was considered rare and endangered in the 1960s, but large numbers of them thrive today on Madeira, Tenerife, La Palma, and Gomera. It is extinct on Grand Canary.

The plain swift. Known for its solid black plumage, the plain swift strongly resembles the barn swallow, but it is smaller. It visits tall cliffs, where it performs high speed acrobatics. Part of the population migrates in winter to more southern zones such as the Cape Verde Islands. The rest of the birds stay in one habitat all year. The plain swift can be observed on Madeira and the western Canaries.

Canarian pipit. This species is much smaller than the common tawny pipit. It is also darker and has more spots on its breast. Pipits prefer open spaces and the volcanic, semi-desert plains. Local people call it *caminero,* or traveler, because of its ability to follow something. It lives at about 9,800 feet (3,000 m) high on Tenerife and is found on all the Canaries, the Selvagens, Madeira, and Porto Santo.

Canarian chat. This species lives on Fuerteventura and the islands of Alegranza and Montaña Clara, which are north of Lanzarote. Ornithologists, however, failed to find it on Alegranza and Montaña Clara in 1970. It is believed that the number of these birds varies greatly at different times. This chat is the most localized and least studied endemic species of the Canaries.

Teydean chaffinch. Slightly larger than the common chaffinch, it is entirely slate blue except for its white belly. The white wing-bands, typical of the chaffinch, have almost entirely disappeared in this species. Teydeans prefer cone-bearing, or coniferous, forests. Two populations have been identified, one on Tenerife and one on Grand Canary. In 1970, ornithologists also observed this species on Lanzarote. It may have migrated to this new habitat because forest replanting on Tererife caused an increase in that bird population. Thus, crowding may have forced some birds to migrate to Lanzarote.

The canary. The Canary Islands are the original home of one of the most famous birds in the world, the canary. The canaries that are raised in cages and aviaries all over the world are very different from their wild ancestors.

Wild canaries are smaller, 4.9 inches (12.5 cm), compared to most of the domestic canaries that can range between 5.5 and 5.9 inches (14 to 15 cm). They generally

On these two pages, the most characteristic marine birds of the region are shown. *From left to right:* the Madeiran storm petrel, Bulwer's petrel, the soft-plumaged petrel, and the white-faced petrel.

have a streaked grayish green back and yellow-green breast and rump. Males are much lighter in color. On the whole, wild canaries look a lot like European finches but are larger and have a more melodious song.

Canaries can be found in a number of environments, as long as trees or bushy vegetation are present. The birds show a particular preference for Canarian pine plantations. Canaries are usually herbivorous, feeding themselves and their young mainly on seeds, grasses, shoots, and other plant substances. In fact, the reason canaries and their chicks are such easy pets to raise is that they thrive on this ordinary diet.

It is believed that these little birds were exported to Europe for the first time in the sixteenth century. They survived and reproduced well in captivity. Their easy care and melodious song made them very popular. Eventually, new varieties appeared. Breeders exploited slight mutations, or differences, which appeared in the breeding stock of the canaries. They carefully chose certain unusual characteristics and bred the canaries so that these unique differences would become more noticeable. As a result, some new strains were developed. The tufted canaries are similar to the *Gloucester*, while giant canaries are like the *York-*

shire and *Norwich*. Canaries with extraordinary songs, canaries with curled plumage, and even humpbacked canaries appeared. By crossing yellow canaries with the red siskin (a South American finch whose plumage is mostly red), rosy and reddish canaries have also been obtained. A visit to a show of these beautiful delicate birds is a truly unique and unforgettable experience.

During its five centuries of domestication, the canary gradually has shed the appearance of its wild ancestors and has become quite a different animal. It has adapted to living in a cage or aviary and probably could not survive on its own in the wild. Breeder associations and clubs are dedicated to the canary. Many books have been written on the successful keeping and breeding of canaries.

Originally, most pets, like cats and dogs, were kept for a practical purpose. The canary, however, is raised only for its beauty and its song. No other pet has been so popular for these reasons. Because of the canary's popularity, some of the beauty and fascination of the Canary Islands has enriched the lives of people all over the world.

GUIDE TO AREAS OF NATURAL INTEREST

The Sahara is crossed more and more often by travelers in cross-country vehicles. Even casual tourists on the Mediterranean coast of North Africa travel in the desert without hesitation at least near the borders.

A trip to North Africa requires some preparation and knowledge, even if it will not include crossing the heart of the Sahara. Light clothing and Saharan style shoes are necessary. Other indispensable equipment includes sunglasses, a hat, water, and a first-aid kit containing sunscreen, anti-scorpion serum, and anti-viper serum.

Car traffic on the desert roads is tightly regulated. Generally, side trips into the desert are classified by degree of risk. Some routes present little danger, while others are definitely dangerous. In some cases, traveling by car may be prohibited. People who travel by auto must observe certain rules. For example, cars may be allowed on the road only in caravans of at least two, and driving at night may be forbidden. In any case, people who drive by themselves into the desert must take a reserve supply of fuel and some basic spare parts for their vehicles. They also must know how to make most of the necessary repairs alone. The traveler must be aware that the Sahara today is still as dangerous as it was when camels were the only means of transportation. Sudden car failure on a lonely route in the summer can rapidly turn an adventure into a tragedy. Unfortunately, events of this kind still happen in the desert.

Today, many excellent paved roads have been built in the Sahara. Because they lead to places rich in fauna, flora, and splendid landscapes, there is no reason to take senseless risks by venturing onto remote and difficult paths. It is important to remember that bathing in the water of rivers or oasis pools is dangerous. A person could contract *schistosomiasis*, a grave sickness caused by a parasitic worm that attacks the uro-genital system.

People who want to camp in tents should bring warm sleeping bags because the desert nights are cold. It is wise to use camp beds or tents that can be mounted on the roofs of vehicles to avoid scorpions and snakes. A thermal bag will be useful to protect photographic film.

The best time to travel in the Sahara is spring or autumn. In the winter, the short days and cold nights make the trip less enjoyable. In summer, the heat is unbearable for some people. The best time for visiting the Atlas Mountains is from late spring to the end of summer. The Canary Islands, Azores, and Madeira are pleasant any time of the year.

Opposite page: A four-wheel drive vehicle travels a paved road of the Great Western Erg (Algeria). Even when the road surface is good, the sand often sweeps over it, making passage difficult for less powerful vehicles.

Right: Highlighted are areas of natural interest in North Africa. National parks established for conservation reasons are rare in the Sahara because the territory is protected by its own harshness and inaccessibility. In this chapter, desert areas, parks of the island groups, and the most interesting humid areas along the Mediterranean are described.

Below: Territories discussed in this volume include the Sahara, the Atlas Mountains, the Mediterranean, Mediterranean coasts of North Africa (humid areas), and island groups such as the Canary, Madeira, and Azores islands.

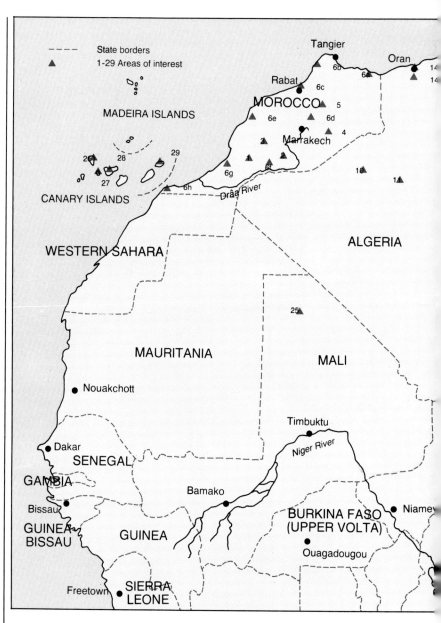

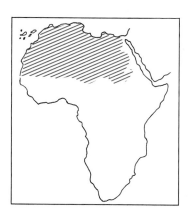

MOROCCO

Tafraoute (1)

In the Low Atlas Mountains, it is very interesting to observe the steppe vegetation as a transition area into the desert. There are many spectacular expanses of spurge (shrubby plants), palm groves, and picturesque heights in this particular area. One of the most interesting excursions begins at Tafraoute, 84 miles (135 km) southeast of Agadir. Tafraoute has splendid granite mountains. The rocks appear in interesting and quite unusual shapes because of wind erosion.

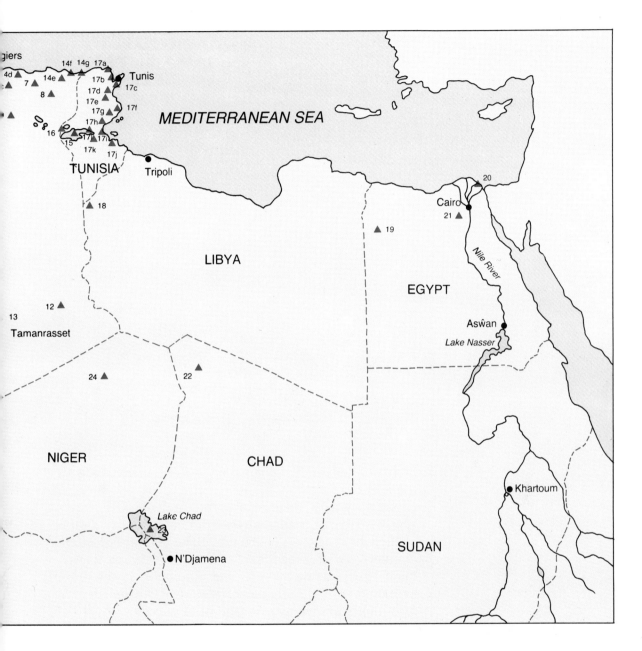

Drâa (2)

High Atlas (3)

The old itinerary of Heim de Balsac can be followed, at least in part, by traveling to Ouarzazate, which lies 127 miles (204 km) from Marrakech. From this point, the route continues to Zagora along the valley of the ancient Drâa River. There are excellent opportunities for observing the Saharan flora and fauna in these areas.

The most interesting area of the entire range is probably the High Atlas National Park. Visitors can view areas of

Pictured is a spectacular view of a mirage in the Ténére Desert (Niger). The "water" seen on the horizon is caused by refraction (light bending as it passes through an obstacle) due to the great heat. The "islands" created by the refraction are actually just the dunes.

high altitude and plateaus, as well as many endemic life-forms.

Among the endemic species are Andreansky's lizard, a species of scarab beetle, and an orthopteron, which is found as high as 13,124 feet (4,000 m). Mixed colonies of Alpine choughs as well as the roller *Coracia pyrrochorax* also live here. They are the most southern colonies in the entire Palearctic region. The center of this area is Oukaimeden, the most important winter ski resort of Morocco.

Ziz (4)

The gorges of Ziz, which means "gazelle" in Berber, can be reached by Meknès-Azrou-Midelt-Er Rachidia Road. They offer beautiful landscapes and wandering paths between limestone and marl (a crumbly calcium rock). Palm groves and the characteristic desert fauna can be seen here.

Azrou (5)

The Azrou Forest is located near Azrou in the Middle Atlas. It has beautiful cedars, oaks, and other trees. The fauna includes the Barbary ape, the leopard, and numerous birds.

(a) *Mouth of the Moulouya River.* This delta environment of lagoons and coastal dunes is located in front of the Chafarinas Islands (east of Melilla), where a large colony of Cory's shearwaters and Audouin's gulls lives. Numerous herons and bitterns, spoonbills, greater flamingos, anatids (ducks, geese, and swans), and members of the Rallidae family (rails, crakes, and coots) winter in the delta environment.

b) *Merja Zerga Reserve.* This area is located on the Atlantic coast south of Larache and is probably the most important humid environment in Morocco. It is a lagoon and occupies 12 sq. miles (30 sq. km). Because a canal connects it with the sea, the water rises and falls with the tides. It is a very important wintering spot for aquatic birds and a resting place for migrators. As many as fifty thousand ducks and forty thousand European coots as well as over one hundred thousand limicolines have been observed here during the winter.

c) *Sidi Bou Rhaba Reserve.* This marsh is located south of the mouth of the Sebou River on the Atlantic coast

Pictured is a nomad traveling with two dromedaries. This age-old means of locomotion in the desert is very slow compared to a car. On the other hand, it is reliable and still used for small trips and for trading purposes.

between Rabat and Kenitra. It is about .62 miles (1 km) from the sea and is separated from the rest of the area by a small dike. Further south is a wide, humid area that varies in size with the seasons. Dunes ring the Merja depression. Marsh turtles, African chameleons, gerbils, brown hares, and rabbits can be found here.

The great crested grebe, night heron, cattle egret, little egret, and the marbled teal also nest here. It is an important location for passing limicolines and a wintering ground for anatids.

d) *Lakes of the Middle Atlas.* These are a group of about eighty small lakes between 2,625 and 3,937 feet (800 to 1,200 m) above sea level. Some of them, like Affenourir Lake, are very interesting and have been included in the Ramsar Agreement for the protection of humid areas. They cover a surface area of 5 sq. miles (14 sq. km). About ten thousand anatids winter here, and such endangered species as the bald ibis, ruddy shelduck, horned coot, and the demoiselle crane nest near these lakes.

e) *Oualidja Lagoon.* Located south of El Jadida, this lagoon covers about 4 sq. miles (10 sq. km). A strip of dune separates Oualidja Lagoon from the sea. In spite of much human activity, it is the third most important humid area in Morocco. A great number of limicolines winter here, and the slender-billed curlew, which is now very rare, has been observed here.

f) *Iriki.* This area includes about 77 sq. miles (200 sq. km). It is south of Ouarzazate and is crossed by a subsidiary of the Drâa River. Many thousands of greater flamingos and hundreds of marbled teals can be observed wintering here. Ruddy shelducks and black-winged stilts can also be observed nesting here.

g) *Mouth of the Massa River.* Located on the Atlantic coast, this area is south of Agadir. Together with other estuaries, it is an important resting place for migrating spoonbills and greater flamingos. It is also a wintering ground for limicolines.

h) *Sebkha Tozra.* This lagoon is located near Puerto Cansado, almost at the border of Mauritania. It is separated from the sea by dunes, which are submerged during high tide. It is the second largest humid area in Morocco after Merja Zerga and is the largest wintering ground for limicolines. On the average, twenty thousand of these birds migrate here. The common tern and the slender-billed gull also nest here.

ALGERIA

Babor (7)

El Abiod (8)

Khonguet El Melah (9)

Beni Abbès (10)

Timimoun (11)

The Djebel Babor is a mountain that is part of the Little Kabylie chain. It is located to the south of the Gulf of Béjaia and is about 12 miles (20 km) from Béjaia Center. It rises to 6,575 feet (2,004 m) above sea level and is characterized by a cool and humid climate. Ninety-eight inches (2,500 mm) of rain fall annually. In the winter, its peaks are snow covered. In the summer, rain is scarce. The vegetation includes cedars, firs, deciduous zeen oaks, yews, poplars, maples, and so on. There are also many endemic plant species.

The most noteworthy animal species is the Kabylian nuthatch, a small perching bird found only on this mountain range. It was identified first in 1975.

South of Constantine, the Aurès Mountains are crossed by a long depression, where layers of rock have sloped downward to form a trough. Here the wadi El Abiod has dug its bed. Splendid palm groves and orchards grow alongside the river. Farther northeast beyond the Tighanimine gorges, the landscape becomes Mediterranean. Holm oaks and cedars grow there. Travelers can drive through the entire area along a very beautiful road leading from Batna to Biskra, where lodgings are available.

On the road betwen Algiers and Laghouat, 15 miles (25 km) north of Djelfa, the *Khonguet El Melah* (salt cliff) rises on the wadi Melah. It is about 4,922 feet (1,500 m) wide and about 328 feet (100 m) high. The salt on the surface comes from the discharge of saline clay by pressure through sedimentary layers.

Beautiful examples of *barchans* (moving, crescent-shaped sand dunes) 49 to 66 feet (15 to 20 m) high can be seen in the Great Western Erg near the village of Beni Abbès, about 435 miles (700 km) southwest of Oran. Beni Abbès is an excellent starting point for an excursion to a typically Saharan environment. Overnight lodging is available.

The Timimoun Oasis is located between the Tademait Plateau and the Great Western Erg. It is one of the best starting points for excursions to areas of *hammada, erg,* and *shott.* Just outside the village is a large water tank. Nearby, a sandy path about 2 miles (4 km) long leads to the petrified forest. Silicified, or rock-like, remains of trees many millions of years old can be seen. Lodging of various kinds is available in the oasis.

Shown is a view of El Jerid shott, the largest salt lake in the Sahara. The vast basin of the shott spreads over 3,088 sq. miles (8,000 sq. km) in southern Tunisia. For the most part, it is covered by a thick salt crust. During the winter, it is partially flooded. During the summer, the water surface gradually shrinks until only small pools remain. The salt crystallizes at the edges of the pools and forms beautiful shapes.

Tassili n'Ajjer (12)

Ahaggar Mountains (13)

Humid zones (14 a-g)

Northeast of the Ahaggar Mountains rise pinnacles and towers that appear sculpted in sandstone. For 600 million years, erosion has eaten away these rocks. As a result, the landscapes are breathtaking. The Djanet Oasis is located in the heart of Tassili. Tassili is an excellent place to lodge and begin exploring the various Saharan environments and rock sculptures. Access is normally from Tamanrasset by a long path.

The Ahaggar Massif is the age-old refuge of the Tuareg people. It is formed by angular, wall-like mountains and covers almost 212,300 sq. miles (550,000 sq. km). The annual precipitation averages only 7 inches (169 mm). Where there are springs, however, a luxuriant oleander underbrush grows. Many examples of *erg, drinn plains,* and bushes in the genus *Salsola* can be found.

The center of the area is Tamanrasset, where lodging and food can be obtained. It is accessible from Algiers by a paved road, which runs for almost 1,240 miles (2,000 km) from the Mediterranean coast to the middle of the desert. Tamanrasset also can be reached more comfortably by plane.

a) *Lake Macta.* It is located west of Oran and covers 13 sq. miles (35 sq. km). About 25,000 ducks winter there.

b) *Oran Sebkha.* This site covers about 386 sq. miles (1,000 sq. km) and is visited in winter by more than 1,000 greater flamingos, 1,000 shelducks, 3,000 gadwalls, 2,500 European coots, and more than 1,000 avocets. It is immediately west of Oran and reached easily from there.

c) *Lake Bougzoul.* This lake is in an arid environment with tamarisk shrubs. It is located 109 miles (175 km) south of Algiers between Boukhari and Aïn Oussera. At least 46 species of aquatic birds winter here. These birds include 3,000 greater flamingos and more than 22,000 ducks. The black-winged stilt, avocet, gull-billed tern, marbled teal, and purple gallinule nest here. In the past, the demoiselle crane (until 1910) and the bald ibis also could be found here.

d) *Reghaia Swamp.* This swamp occupies a total surface of less than 1 sq. mile (2.3 sq. km). It is located about 19 miles (30 km) east of Algiers at the estuary of the Reghaia River. Though it is small, it is alive with many interesting species of birds. The marbled teal, purple gallinule, little bittern, and others come to nest. The area also is used as an autumn resting place by 700 to 800 egrets.

114

e) *Lake Fetzara.* Located southwest of Annaba and covering 58 sq. miles (150 sq. km), this lake is an important wintering ground for birds like lapwings and the greater golden plover.

f) *Plain of Gerbes.* Located east of Annaba on 193 sq. miles (500 sq. km), this region is crossed by the El Kebir River. It is accessible only by foot. Greylag geese, spur-winged plovers, and snipes winter here.

g) *El Kala Ponds.* El Kala is a small village near the Tunisian border. It is surrounded by six small lakes and lagoons that cover a total of about 77 sq. miles (200 sq. km). Many ducks (about one million wigeons) and geese winter here along with other aquatic birds.

TUNISIA

El Djerid (15)

This huge saline depression covers 2,702 sq. miles (7,000 sq. km) and is the largest and one of the most accessible *shotts* (salt deserts) in North Africa. Travelers crossing the 50 miles (80 km) that stretch between Tozeur and Kebili can see spectacular landscapes, mirages, oases, and other desert scenery. Far from the road, a large colony of greater flamingos nests inside the shott. Lodging is available in Tozeur or Nefta.

Nefta (16)

Eight artesian springs give life to this spendid oasis located in southern Tunisia. It has 380,000 palms that produce the well-known *deglat-nour* (fingers of light) dates. The oasis is located near the shott El Jerid and is easily accessible by car from Tunis via Gafsa. Reasonably good lodging is available.

Humid zones (17 a-l)

a) *Estuary of the Medjerda River.* This waterway occupies 29 sq. miles (75 sq. km) of unprotected land. It can be reached from Aousdja, which lies between Bizerte and Tunis. The Medjerda is the largest river in Tunisia and flows into the Mediterranean. It forms many lagoons where it meets the sea. There are 33,000 aquatic birds in the area. Most of them are ducks (wigeons, pintails, and shovelers), though limicolines (5,000 to 10,000) winter here along with cranes.

b) *Lake Ichkeul.* This lake is in a humid area of 46 sq. miles (120 sq. km) near Bizerte. Aquatic birds, including the rare marbled teal and the purple gallinule, nest here. More than 10,000 greylag geese, 150,000 ducks (wigeons, pochards, teals, shovelers, and some white-headed ducks), and more

Shown are the oasis and village of Beni Abbès in Algeria. The oases survived long ago because people grew thousands of date palms there. Today, oases continue to be developed because of modern economic projects such as oil drilling. These fertile spots in the desert will be even more important in the future of the desert people.

than 150,000 European coots winter here.

c) *Lake Tunis.* Many birds come to winter in this area, which covers 23 sq. miles (60 sq. km). Some of the birds seen here include 2,000 to 3,000 cormorants, 5,000 greater flamingos, 20,000 ducks (mostly pochards, but also hundreds of white-headed ducks), 20,000 European coots, and 10,000 limicolines.

d) *Sebkha Es-Sejoumi.* This spot is most important as a wintering ground for 25,000 greater flamingos and 10,0000 shelducks. Thousands of ducks and limicolines winter here, and the marbled teal nests here irregularly.

e) *Sebkha El Kelbia.* Located to the north of Kairouran, this flat, arid environment covers 54 sq. miles (140 sq. km). Many ducks (up to 270,000) and European coots winter here. As many as 5,000 cranes stop to feed in the area, and many aquatic birds nest here.

f) *Sebkha Sidi El Hani.* Thousands of greater flamingos occasionally nest in this area that occupies 135 sq. miles (350 sq. km) south of Sousse.

g) *Sebkha El Jem.* This sebkha is 12 sq. miles (30 sq. km) of brackish water between Sousse and Sfax. It is a wintering ground for over 30,000 European coots, thousands of limicolines, greater flamingos, shelducks, shovelers, black-necked grebes, and others. Greater flamingos, white-headed ducks, marbled teals, black-winged stilts, avocets, collared pranticoles, slender-billed gulls, and gull-billed terns nest on the islets in the area.

h) *Saline of Thyna.* This small area is located near the Thyna Center south of Sfax. Hundreds of greater flamingos, a thousand spoonbills, and thousands of limicolines winter here. Birds such as the redshank, common tern, and the lesser crested tern also nest here.

i) *Coast opposite the Kneiss Islands.* This strip is located between Nakta and La Sakhira in the Gulf of Gabès. Over a hundred thousand limicolines, spoonbills, and cormorants winter here.

j) *Lagoon of Bahiret El Bibane.* Various limicolines, gulls, and cormorants come to this area south of Jerba to spend their winters.

k) *National Park of Bou Hedma, Sebkha Mansour, and En-Noual.* This park is located inland about 116 sq. miles (300 sq. km) between Sakhira and Gabès. Thousands of ducks (teals, pintails, pochards, and sometimes ferrugineous, or rust-colored, ducks and white-headed ducks), over 25,000 European coots, and hundreds of cranes winter here.

l) *Lake El Fejai and Sebkha El Hamma.* This brackish depression that lies east of the shott El Jerid is very important as a wintering ground. It is also a very important nesting site for greater flamingos. About 8,000 pairs were observed in 1974.

LIBYA

Ghadāmis (18)

The oasis of Ghadāmis, called "the pearl of the desert," is located 373 miles (600 km) southwest of Tripoli. It can be reached by plane or paved road. Along the road, Al Hammā dah Al Hamrā, the rocky desert near Sīnāwin and Dirj, and the sand dunes near Ramlat Al Bab can be admired. Other important Libyan oases that can be seen are Sabhā, Murzuq, and Al Kufrah.

EGYPT

Siwa (19)

The oasis of Siwa lies deep in the Libyan-Egyptian desert in a depression about 98 feet (30 m) below sea level and more than 186 miles (300 km) southwest of Marsa Matrûh. It is an excellent location for travelers to observe the typical Saharan fauna as well as the ancient Egyptian temples.

Burullus (20)

This lagoon of the Nile delta spreads over about 135 sq. miles (350 sq. km) in a partially cultivated, partly dune-like environment. This area is known for birds such as anatids and limicolines, which pass through. These birds may also winter there. The most convenient access is from Baltim. It is also possible to find lodgings at Baltim.

Qârûn (21)

Lake Qârûn is located at the oasis of El Faiyûm, 60 miles (96 km) south of Cairo. It can be reached by a good road passing through Ibshwāi. This lake has an average depth of only 13 feet (4 m), and many aquatic birds winter there. In the surrounding area live gazelles, black-bellied sand grouses, and many other desert animals. Lodgings are available at the oasis.

CHAD

Tibesti (22)

Following pages: A beautiful landscape of salt and rocks near the Terjhit Oasis in Mauritania is pictured.

These mountains are located in one of the most remote regions of Africa. This war-torn area has spectacular valleys, volcanic landscapes, rock carvings, and oases rich in Saharan flora and fauna. During war, it is necessary to obtain a special permit from the government of Chad to visit.

119

Chad (23)

A relict of an ancient inland sea, Lake Chad now occupies over 3,860 sq. miles (10,000 sq. km). On its surface, numerous floating islands can be seen.

Niger

Ténére (24)

Located west of Agadez and about 435 miles (700 km) beyond Tamanrasset, the Ténére is one of the most remote and unexplored regions of the Sahara. About twenty years ago, a real dinosaur graveyard was discovered there.

Mali

Taoudenni (25)

Located deep in the desert about 435 miles (700 km) north of Timbuktu, the salt mine of Taoudenni is located on an island many miles long. Today, it is a penal colony, and no one is allowed to enter.

Canary Islands

Taburiente (26)

The caldera (crater) of Taburiente, center of the national park with the same name, is the collapsed cone of a volcano. It has formed a very large crater that reaches 7,950 feet (2,423 m) in height and occupies the central part of the island of São Miguel de la Palma.

Garajonay (27)

Located in the center of the small island of Gomera, the National Park of Garajonay is important because it protects the most beautiful laurel forest left on the archipelago.

Teide (28)

This ancient volcano is 12,199 feet (3,718 m) high. Today, it is the heart of the Teide National Park, which occupies 50 sq. miles (130 sq. km) on the island of Tenerife.

Timanfaya (29)

There are fantastic volcanic landscapes with expanses of lava, craters with scarce vegetation, as well as animals in this national park on Lanzarote.

Azores

These volcanic islands swept by Atlantic winds are well worth a visit for their spectacular landscapes. They also display rich, native, and cultivated plant life. Animal life on the islands is similar to European fauna. The varied marine life includes tuna, swordfish, barracuda, and various whales, which are still hunted today. Using the traditional method, local fishermen in boats throw the harpoons by hand.

GLOSSARY

aglyph a snake with solid fangs.

alkaloid any of a number of substances containing nitrogen and usually oxygen occurring especially in seed plants.

Allen's rule desert animals have larger legs, tails, and ears than similar species in cooler regions, which help rid them of excess heat.

amphibian an organism that lives both on land and in water.

arachnid a class of arthropods including scorpions, spiders, mites, and ticks.

archipelago a group of islands

arthropod a group of invertebrates with jointed bodies and limbs and an outer shell.

Bacterian camel a species of camel that has two humps.

bedouins nomadic Arabs of the Syrian, Arabian, and North African deserts.

biogeography the study of the geographic distribution of plants and animals.

biological clock a built-in timing mechanism responsible for various cyclic behaviors, such as regular migration, in living beings.

carnivore meat-eating animal.

ciconiiformes an order of birds that includes herons, storks, ibises, and spoonbills.

crassulacae acid metabolism (CAM) a kind of photosynthesis occuring in the dark, needing light only in the last stages.

crustacean a class of mostly aquatic, segmented arthopods with outer skeletons, such as lobsters and crabs.

cryptic coloration coloration that allows an organism to blend in with its surroundings; camouflage.

cuticles external, protective layers of a plant's stem.

cyanic acid a strong acid used to prepare salts.

deciduous plants whose leaves fall at the end of the growing season.

deflation the action of the wind that erodes soil.

dehydration loss of moisture.

delta a fanlike deposit of soil at the mouth of a river.

diurnal active during the day.

dorsal situated on or near the back.

dromedary a species of camel that has one hump.

exoskeleton a skeleton on the outside of an organism.

fascia connecting tissues of the abdomen.

felids members of the cat, or feline, family.

granivorous feeding mainly on seeds and grains.

gregarious tending to associate with others of one's kind.

heliotrium a group of herbs or shrubs whose flowers turn toward the sun.

herbivore a plant-eating animal.

herpetology the study of amphibians and reptiles.

holarctic region the northern parts of the Eastern and Western hemispheres.

Hymenoptera an order of insects that includes wasps, ants, and bees.

Hysosciamus falezlez a poisonous Old World herb.

insecticide a substance used to control or eliminate insects.

insectivorous insect-eating organisms.

Jacobson's organ a sense organ of reptiles used to smell tiny particles they pick up with their tongues.

lamella a thin, flat scale, membrane, or part; (pl. lamellae).

larva the immature, wingless form that hatches from the egg of many insects; (pl. larvae).

legume a plant having nitrogen-fixing bacteria in the roots, such as pea and bean.

Mediterranean climate one characterized by cold, wet winters and dry, hot summers.

Mesozoic era a period in the earth's history from 65 to 230 million years ago.

metabolic water water in the body of an organism that is used for life processes.

metabolize chemical changes in living cells by which energy is provided for life processes.

nocturnal active at night.

opisthoglyph a snake with long, grooved fangs.

ornithology the study of birds.

oxidization the process by which a substance combines with oxygen.

Palearctic northern nondesert regions of Africa.

pedipalp a hairy appendage growing near the mouth of an arachnid, such as a spider.

perennial a plant that survives for several seasons producing flowers.

photosynthesis the formation of carbohydrates in plants exposed to light.

physiology the study of how organisms function in life.

precipitation moisture that falls in the form of rain, snow, hail, or mist.

proteroglyph a snake with a pair of grooved fangs in front of the upper jaw.

rhizome a horizontal plant stem.

saurian a group containing lizards and crocodiles.

savanna a grassy plain with clusters of trees growing here and there.

schistosomiasis an illness caused by a parasitic worm that attacks the urogenital system.

solenoglyph a snake with fangs in the front of the jaw.

stomata the pores of leaves.

Tertiary period a period in the earth's history between 2 and 65 million years ago.

torpor a state of being inactive and stiff.

tubule a slender, long channel in the body of an organism.

uric acid a white, odorless, and tasteless acid present in the urine of mammals.

xerophyte a plant adapted for life and growth with a limited water supply.

INDEX

CREDITS

MAPS AND DRAWINGS. G. Vaccaro, Cologna Veneta (VR). **PHOTOGRAPHS. E. Biasin,** Verona: 64-65. **A. Borroni,** Milan: M. Mairani 112-113. **A. Carapezza,** Palermo: 94. **A. Casdia,** Brugherio (MI): sovraccoperta, 16, 24-25, 34, 39, 58, 67, 68, 80-81. **Diamonde,** Turin: F. Arcolin 89; A Bacchella 17,21, 48; Archivio Diamonde 8. **E. Duelevant,** Turin: 35. **Equipe Kel 12,** Mestre (VE): 12-13, 14-15, 20, 22-23, 40, 108-109, 116-117. **B. Massa,** Palermo: 71. **G. Massa,** Montecarlo: 70, 84. **Overseas,** Milan: Oxford Scientific Films/J. and D. Bartlett 54; Jacana/J.L.S. Dubois 61; Jacana/J.P. Varin 53. **Panda Photo.** Rome: G. Cagnucci 97; A. Petretti 29, 83; F. Petretti 32, 42-43,44; F. Pratesi 50-51; R. Sigismondi 30; WWF International/T. Grpinar 85. **L. Pellegrini,** Milan: 74-75. **L. Ricciarini,** Milan: N. Cirani 18, 72-73, 78, 106-107, 120-121. **M.P. Stradella,** Milan: studio Pizzi 6-7, 46, 86. **Union Press,** Milan: G. Gualco 27, 36-37, 90-91. **F. Veronesi,** Segrate (MI): 59.

REFERENCE--NOT TO BE
TAKEN FROM THIS ROOM

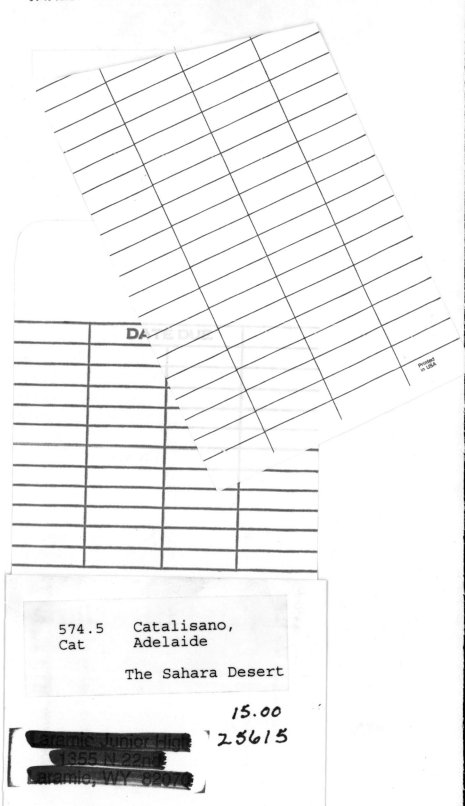

DATE DUE

Printed in USA

574.5   Catalisano,
Cat   Adelaide

          The Sahara Desert

                              15.00
Laramie Junior High   25615
1355 N. 22nd
Laramie, WY 82070